THE ULTIMATE
BOSTON RED SOX
TRIVIA BOOK

A Collection of Amazing Trivia Quizzes
and Fun Facts for Die-Hard BoSox Fans!

Ray Walker

Exclusive Free Book
Crazy Sports Stories

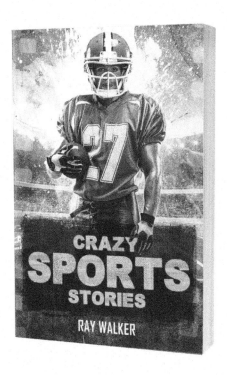

CONTENTS

INTRODUCTION

Obviously, you're inspired by your favorite team. In this case, the team in lights is none other than the Boston Red Sox, one of the original franchises in the American League, and surely, one of the best ever in the entire glorious history of Major League Baseball (Although, archrival New York Yankees fans might want to argue over your claim just a bit.).

The city of Boston has always been filled with winning pro teams: the inimitable Boston Celtics and their eight straight championships, the Bruins flying around the ice in Boston Garden, and, more recently, the New England Patriots, winning everything in sight in both Foxboro and Gillette Stadium.

But the Boston Red Sox are extra special. There's no place to play hardball in the world like their home park, Fenway. In fact, it's now the oldest stadium in existence in MLB, and it comes complete with a massive left-field wall called "the Green Monster" (And there are even some choice seats available on top, for a price (!), as you're about to find out in this book.).

Next year, the Boston Red Sox will celebrate 120 years of

existence at (or near!) the peak of the baseball world, and you'll be there, armed with all the trivia and fun facts on their colorful players, big signings and trades, and the incredible emotional highs and lows of a world championship team. The Red Sox have had more than their fair share. The team has a connection with one of baseball's truly unique legends, "the Curse of the Bambino," as well as the 9/11 World Trade Center attacks and the Boston Marathon bombing. But we all must overcome, and there are many more merrier moments, like World Series wins in 2004, 2007, 2013, and 2018, to quiz your friends and family on.

Clearly, you may use the book as you wish. Each chapter contains 20 quiz questions that are a mix of multiple-choice, true-false formats, an answer key (Don't worry, it's on a separate page!), and a section of ten "Did You Know?" factoids about the team.

And for the record, the information and stats in this book are current up to the beginning of 2020. The BoSox will surely break more records and win many more awards as the seasons march on, so keep this in mind when you're watching the next game with your friends. You never quite know: someone could suddenly start a conversation with the phrase "Did you know...?", and you'll be ready.

CHAPTER 1:

ORIGINS & HISTORY

QUIZ TIME!

1. The Boston Red Sox play baseball in Fenway Park, the oldest baseball stadium in North America. When was it inaugurated?

    a. 1900

    b. 1910

    c. 1912

    d. 1922

2. Way back when, in their first-ever Fenway game, Boston faced a team that would later change its name to the Yankees. What was that team's original name?

    a. Rangers

    b. Bronxers

    c. Yonkers

    d. Highlanders

3. Before the left-field fence in Fenway was called "the Green Monster," what was its initial name?

a. The Wall

b. The Great Divide

c. The Moat

d. The Fierce Fence

4. The Green Monster also hosts the only manually operated scoreboard in the Major Leagues. How many slots does it have for the score and other stats?

    a. 100

    b. 27

    c. 57

    d. 127

5. In fact, the Green Monster has a few choice seats on top of it, if you care to pay the price. How many does it have to be exact?

    a. 269

    b. 1,912

    c. 555

    d. 1,000

6. One nickname for the Boston Red Sox is BoSox, used to distinguish them from the Chicago White Sox or ChiSox. Which of the following is NOT another BoSox nickname?

    a. The Crimson Tide

    b. The Red Sox Nation

    c. The Cardiac Kids

    d. The Crimson Hose

7. During one disastrous stretch, the Red Sox didn't win a single championship for decades on end (Luckily, that was

last century, the twentieth!). Which player did the Sox trade that brought on the so-called "curse"?

a. Wade Boggs
b. Joe DiMaggio
c. Babe Ruth
d. Jim Rice

8. Which other team besides Boston suffered an even longer championship drought?

a. Philadelphia Phillies
b. Chicago Cubs
c. Baltimore Orioles
d. New York Yankees

9. The Red Sox ultimately blasted out of the dreaded drought in 2004. Who was their unlucky victim in the World Series that year?

a. Houston Astros
b. Milwaukee Brewers
c. St. Louis Cardinals
d. Los Angeles Dodgers

10. Boston fans tried everything to stop "the Curse of the Bambino" and bring a championship back to Fenway Park. All of the actions below were attempted EXCEPT one:

a. Fans searched for a buried piano at Babe Ruth's old farmhouse.
b. One fan burned a Yankees cap at the bottom of Mt. Everest (while placing an intact Boston cap at the summit!).

c. A ship painted in Yankee colors was ceremoniously sunk in Boston Harbor.

d. "Witches" were hired to try to break the curse.

11. Before 1920 (and the infamous curse), the Red Sox had won five championships, and the Yankees hadn't won any.

    a. True

    b. False

12. Just before being traded from Boston to New York in 1920, "the Babe" set a World Series record in 1918 that stood for 43 years for:

    a. 29 straight scoreless innings as a pitcher

    b. 21 consecutive strikeouts as a pitcher

    c. four home runs (also called round-trippers) in the same game as a batter

    d. batting for the cycle (a single, double, triple, and home run in the same game) twice in one series of games

13. When Boston battled to beat "the Curse," they reached Game 7 of the 1946 Series, only to have an opponent score from first on a single to sink the Sox. Who was the player?

    a. Eddie Lake for Detroit

    b. Enos Slaughter for St. Louis

    c. Jackie Robinson for Brooklyn

    d. Pat Seerey for Cleveland

14. The aforementioned run in 1946 against the Sox was so unlikely, it gained a famous name. What was it?

a. The Mad Dash

b. The Sad Score

c. The Rabbit Run

d. The Terrible Tally

15. In 1967, the BoSox earned another snazzy nickname with their first winning campaign since 1958. What was the season called?

a. The Dream Team

b. The Impossible Dream

c. The Sweet '67 Season

d. The Sweet Dream Season

16. Before the turn of the twentieth century, the Red Sox had several unofficial names. Which of the following was one of them?

a. The Red Bats

b. The Red Birds

c. The Red Caps

d. The Red Dogs

17. Just before the 1907 season, another team nickname was briefly used related to the history of the city of Boston. What was it?

a. The Pilgrims

b. The Southies

c. The Tea Partyers

d. The Wanderers

18. Before Boston changed its name to the Red Sox in 1908, which fan club were they supported by?

a. The Boston Bleacher Club

b. The Boston Fan Faction

c. The Royal Rowdies

d. The Royal Rooters

19. The undying spirit of Red Sox fans lives on, even in other cities and "hostile" territories like New York. Where's their base in the Big Apple?

a. Dead Rabbit Grocery & Grog, Financial District

b. Gowanus Gardens, Brooklyn

c. Riviera Café, West Village

d. Underground Cocktail Bar, Chelsea

20. After Babe Ruth was sold to New York, the Boston team struggled with eight straight sub-par seasons from 1925 to 1932. What was their rock-bottom record in '32?

a. 35-119

b. 43-111

c. 49-105

d. 53-101

QUIZ ANSWERS

1. C – 1912
2. D – Highlanders
3. A – The Wall
4. D – 127
5. A – 269
6. A – The Crimson Tide
7. C – Babe Ruth
8. B – Chicago Cubs (108 years)
9. C – St. Louis Cardinals
10. C – A ship painted in Yankee colors was ceremoniously sunk in Boston Harbor.
11. A – True
12. A – 29 straight scoreless innings as a pitcher
13. B – Enos Slaughter for St. Louis
14. A – The Mad Dash
15. B – The Impossible Dream
16. C – The Red Caps
17. A – The Pilgrims
18. D – The Royal Rooters
19. C – Riviera Café, West Village
20. B – 43-111

DID YOU KNOW?

1. The official reason for Babe Ruth's 1920 trade to the Yankees: Boston owner Harry Frazee needed to finance a Broadway musical. The real reason Frazee unloaded Babe? He turned into a home run hitter (and demanded a higher salary), and simultaneously, he disdained pitching. Finally, Frazee (deep in debt) and the Sox struggled with pitiful attendance.

2. Still with Boston, before the big trade, Babe Ruth's gambling habits led him to blow almost all his yearly salary in a few weeks. The BoSox took to paying him on a "per diem basis," and his short-term cash flow improved.

3. When did Boston take the field for the first time? In 1901, when they were called the Boston Americans (and the Pilgrims). Their first championship came after only two years, in 1903, in the first "modern" World Series: they beat the Pittsburgh Pirates, five games to three (clearly different from today's seven-game finale).

4. The first game played in Fenway Park was on April 20, 1912. It was overshadowed by the shocking news of the Titanic sinking on its maiden voyage days before, on April 12. On top of that, the Sox first Fenway affair was postponed three times due to bad weather.

5. When the Red Sox finally kicked things off in Fenway against the New York Highlanders, the ceremonial first

pitch was tossed by Boston mayor, John "Honey Fitz" Fitzgerald. Decades later, it so happened that the mayor's grandson, John F. Kennedy, became the 35th president of the United States.

6. The Boston owner is the Fenway Sports Group, which also controls the Premier League's Liverpool F.C. Boston is a top draw when it travels; only its small home stadium prevents them from leading MLB in overall attendance. Boston sold out every home game it played for ten straight years, from 2003-2013 (820 consecutive games), a major professional sports record.

7. The iconic movie *Fever Pitch* was filmed during the Red Sox 2004 run to an improbable upset of the Yankees (after trailing three games to zero in the ALCS). Fans saw actors Drew Barrymore and Jimmy Fallon making out on the St. Louis diamond as Boston wrapped up the World Series to crush the 86-year-old curse.

8. During the 2004 comeback against New York, Boston ace Curt Schilling was stitched together by a team doctor, allowing him to take the mound and baffle Yankee batters. Close-up cameras showed blood on Schilling's ankle. Fans didn't know at the time, but Morgan practiced the surgery on a cadaver beforehand.

9. "The Curse" began in 1920. But the Red Sox-Yankees rivalry hasn't let up for more than a century. Red Sox star Ted Williams became the first to bat better than .400 in 1941, but Yank Joe DiMaggio got the American League

11

MVP that year for his 56-game hitting streak. Stranger yet: the two players were almost traded a couple years later, but the deal fell through.

10. September 10, 2001: the Boston-New York game was rained out. The next day, the 9/11 attacks devastated New York City. Forgetting their rivalry, Boston fans and players joined in song to honor their stricken neighbors. Alas, the brotherhood did not continue; Boston president Larry Lucchino called the Yankees the "Evil Empire" in 2002.

CHAPTER 2:

WHAT'S IN A NAME?

QUIZ TIME!

1. Which Sox broadcaster, and former player, coined the nickname for larger-than-life slugger David "Big Papi" Ortiz?

   a. Ken Harrelson
   b. Joe Castiglione
   c. Dave O'Brien
   d. Jerry Remy

2. One of the greatest hitters of all time, "Yaz" broke almost every Boston batting record and played only for the Beantowners during his 23-year career. How was his last name really spelled?

   a. Yazztremski
   b. Yastrzemski
   c. Yaztrzemski
   d. Yaztremski

3. Thomas A. Yawkey owned the Red Sox from 1933 until he died in 1976. Under him, the team was the last to integrate in 1959, fully 12 years after Jackie Robinson joined the Brooklyn Dodgers. In 2018, the city of Boston decided to change the Fenway address from Yawkey Way to:

   a. Red Sox Road
   b. Back Bay Way
   c. Freedom Way
   d. Jersey Street

4. Nomar Garciaparra, one of Boston's best shortstops, never won the World Series with Boston, as he was sadly traded away three months before the historic 2004 triumph. Which famous soccer star did he end up marrying?

   a. Michelle Akers
   b. Mia Hamm
   c. Kristine Lilly
   d. Tisha Hoch

5. The name for Fenway Park came from the "fens" or marshlands that were filled in to create the parkland where the vintage stadium now sits.

   a. True
   b. False

6. Writer Bill Nowlin claims the term "Red Sox Nation" originated in 1967 with Boston's improbable run to the Series, only to lose to the Cardinals in Game 7. Nowlin also wrote a book on "Mr. Red Sox," who was:

a. Babe Ruth
b. Bobby Doerr
c. Johnny Damon
d. Johnny Pesky

7. Over the years, the Red Sox have had the knack of picking up top-notch international stars to bolster their ranks. Which of the following BoSox did NOT come from the Dominican Republic?

a. David Ortiz
b. Pedro Martinez
c. Manny Ramírez
d. Luis Tiant

8. Boston's Rico Petrocelli, third baseman from 1963-1976, used a short form of his original first name, which was:

a. Americo
b. Richard
c. Ricardo
d. Federico

9. Which of these nicknames was NOT attributed to the one and only Babe Ruth?

a. The King of Crash
b. The Behemoth of Bust
c. The Big Bang Theory
d. The Sultan of Swat

10. Although he was arguably most famous for his decisive role in the "Bloody Sock Game" versus the Yankees in the

2004 ALCS, Curt Schilling earned a different nickname in Philly: "Red Light." Why?

a. He received numerous tickets for running red traffic lights.

b. He was always looking to talk to the nearest camera.

c. The coaches never allowed him to run if he got on base.

d. He complained he was constantly stuck in Philly traffic.

11. One flame-throwing Red Sox pitcher from 1901-1908 is responsible for the award now given to MLB's best hurler. Who was he?

a. Sly Young

b. Sidney Young

c. Cy Young

d. Denton Blue

12. After the Boston Red Sox won the World Series in 2013, pitcher Jake Peavy bought the vehicle that carried him and teammate Jon Lester in their victory parade, to commemorate his first World Series. What kind of vehicle was it?

a. Fire truck

b. Double-decker bus

c. Duck boat

d. Banana boat

13. One Boston fielder allowed the ball to go between his legs, letting the Mets back into the 1986 Series, and eventually

perpetuating the "Curse of the Bambino." Who was the unfortunate player?

a. Wade Boggs

b. Bill Buckner

c. Roger Clemens

d. Spike Owen

14. The Red Sox not only have an imposing left-field fence affectionately called the Green Monster, but they also have a mascot who lives there. What's his name?

a. Weeping Willie

b. The Monster Green Sock

c. The Green Gorilla

d. Wally the Green Monster

15. Despite his outstanding record as the 2018 Series-winning Red Sox skipper, Alex Cora did not win the "American League Manager of the Year" award. Which one of the following BoSox managers did NOT win either?

a. Dick Williams

b. Butch Hobson

c. Darrell Johnson

d. John McNamara

16. In 1978, the Yankees went on a late-season tear and forced a one-game tiebreaker with the Red Sox in Fenway. What was the light-hitting Yank's name who put the final nail in the Sox coffin that day?

a. Ducky Dilton

b. Hideki Matsui

    c. Bucky Dent

    d. Reggie Jackson

17. Fans might expect to find lots of New England specialties to chomp on during Sox games. Can you name one of the most popular food items that somehow includes the name of a dreaded rival?

    a. New York Bagel Combo

    b. Pin-Stripe Pretzel

    c. Bronx Burger

    d. Yankee Lobster Roll

18. The full name of 2018 Red Sox star outfielder is Markus Lynn Betts, while his nickname is "Mookie." His parents gave him that name so his initials would be "M.L.B.," the same as Major League Baseball.

    a. True

    b. False

19. Besides the illustrious Babe, there were several other prominent BoSox names who were traded to their rivals and went on to win the World Series with New York. Which player below did NOT?

    a. Wade Boggs

    b. Roger Clemens

    c. Johnny Damon

    d. Freddy Lynn

20. Debuting with the Red Sox in 1908, Tristram "Tris" Speaker became known as one of the greatest two-way,

which means good at both fielding and hitting, centerfielders of all time. What was his nickname?

a. The Bald Eagle
b. The Gray Eagle
c. The Fish Hawk
d. The Bird of Prey

QUIZ ANSWERS

1. D – Jerry Remy

2. B – Yastrzemski

3. D – Jersey Street

4. B – Mia Hamm

5. A – True

6. D – Johnny Pesky

7. D – Luis Tiant, He was from Cuba.

8. A – Americo

9. C – The Big Bang Theory

10. B – He was always looking to talk to the nearest camera.

11. C – Cy Young, Though his name at birth was Denton True Young, the Cy Young Award honors the best pitcher.

12. C – Duck boat

13. B – Bill Buckner

14. D – Wally the Green Monster

15. B – Butch Hobson

16. C – Bucky Dent

17. D – Yankee Lobster Roll

18. A – True

19. D – Freddy Lynn

20. B – The Gray Eagle

DID YOU KNOW?

1. The name *Red Sox*, chosen by owner John Taylor, refers to the team uniform's red hose starting in 1908. *Sox* was previously used by newspapers for the Chicago White Sox seeking a headline-friendly form of *Stockings*: "Stockings Win!" just didn't fit in a large-type column.

2. When the Red Sox and Yankees faced off in 1912, some of the actual names in both lineups included: Birdie, Cozy, Duffy, Dutch, Ezra, Gabby, Hack, Heinie, Hick, Hippo, Homer, Iron, Klondike, Olaf, Pinch, Red, Smoky, and Tris.

3. Most fans know that Babe Ruth's 1918 sale from the Sox to the Yanks was the start of an 86-year skid for the Boston squad. Most aren't aware that the Orioles first unloaded Ruth to Boston in 1914 as part of a fire sale by O's owner Jack Dunn, himself drowning in debt due to another Baltimore franchise in the fledgling Federal League.

4. After first patrolling center field with the Sox, Tris Speaker went on to play with the Washington Senators. In 1926, he was accused of "fixing" games together with the great Ty Cobb. Both stars were later cleared by Commissioner Landis and allowed to re-sign.

5. Current Boston slugger Rafael Devers, originally from the Dominican Republic, takes the nickname "Carita" in Spanish, which means "Baby Face," as he was always

smiling as a baby. Silky-smooth shortstop Xander Bogaerts, from Aruba, is known more simply as "X-Man."

6. From 1982-1989, Dennis Ray "Oil Can" Boyd took the mound for the Red Sox. His nickname apparently came from his playing (and beer-drinking) days in hometown Meridian, Mississippi, where beer was coolly known as "oil."

7. During his long and colorful career, Babe Ruth made the move from the Boston Red Sox to the New York Yankees and finally to another Boston team named the Braves (the forerunner of the current Atlanta outfit). He also picked up no fewer than 23 nicknames along the way, including "the Kid of Crash" (He became a pro at the tender age of 19.).

8. "The Curse of the Bambino" was such an integral part of Boston culture for so long that city officials allowed a Longfellow Bridge "Reverse Curve" sign that was graffitied to say "Reverse the Curse" to continue standing until 2004.

9. Called up by the Sox in 1971, Luis Tiant went on to become a successful pitcher and one of the most cherished of all Sox by the fans. His nickname was "El Tiante," which he also lent to a brand of Cuban cigars he endorsed.

10. Red Sox catcher Carlton Fisk is most famous for waving and willing his home run to stay fair to beat the Cincinnati Reds in Game 6 of the 1975 Series. He had two nicknames to choose from behind the plate: "The Commander" or "Pudge."

CHAPTER 3:

FAMOUS QUOTES

QUIZ TIME!

1. Which famous Boston batter was quoted as saying, "All I want out of life is when I walk down the street, folks will say, 'There goes the greatest hitter who ever lived.'"

   a. David Ortiz

   b. Jim Rice

   c. George "Boomer" Scott

   d. Ted Williams

2. Boston once had a unique pitcher named Bill "Spaceman" Lee to whom many hilarious quotes were attributed. In fact, he once said: "Baseball is simple. All you do is sit on your butt, spit tobacco, and nod at the stupid things your manager says."

   a. True

   b. False

3. Carlton Fisk proved to be a rock behind Boston's home plate for years. In the process, he was badly injured

numerous times. How would you complete his telling quote: "If a human body recognized agony and frustration, people would never_____, have babies or play baseball."?

   a. Participate in triathlons

   b. Pull all-nighters

   c. Run marathons

   d. Drive all night

4. When Gabe Kaplan was asked if he made the right decision to leave the Red Sox to play in another country, he quipped, "I have not had second thoughts. I skipped right past second and have had third, fourth, fifth and so on." Which country had he gone to?

   a. South Korea

   b. Japan

   c. Mexico

   d. Taiwan

5. Which minor league affiliate of Boston was Glenn Hoffman talking about when he was sent packing after a spell with the Sox and said, "It's a much bigger city on the way up than it is on the way down."?

   a. Pawtucket, RI

   b. Portland, ME

   c. Salem, VA

   d. Greenville, SC

6. Amazingly, Gene Conley played for three pro teams in the same city: the Boston Braves, the NBA's Boston Celtics,

and finally the Red Sox. What did he compare Fenway Park to when asked about his feeling while pitching there?

    a. A rat trap
    b. A bird cage
    c. A phone booth
    d. A matchbox

7. Dominican pitcher Pedro Martinez twirled a number of fine innings and seasons for the Sox. Besides his fabled right arm, what other body part did he cite for his success?

    a. His brain
    b. His back
    c. His leg
    d. His index finger

8. When Curt Schilling cracked, "I can't throw one, so I bought one." What was he referring to?

    a. Curveball, his canary
    b. Fastball, his cat
    c. Knuckleball, his hamster
    d. Slider, his dog

9. Despite winning more often than not in his tenure with the Sox, "Big Papi" Ortiz tasted defeat a few times as well. What did he say to temper the fans on those occasions?

    a. "You can't drink champagne every day."
    b. "It's not always going to be roses or flowers."
    c. "Life is not just a bowl of cherries."
    d. "The sun doesn't always shine in Boston."

10. When king-sized David Ortiz was selected yet again to test for steroids, what did he tell the media the authorities would most likely find?

    a. A lot of rice and beans
    b. A rack of pork ribs
    c. Everything but the kitchen sink
    d. Nothing but his mom's home cooking

11. At one point, the press hounded Big Papi about finding a way he could bat better against lefties. What word or phrase did he repeat five times, together with "good luck," to reveal his new method?

    a. Confidence
    b. Focus
    c. Swing
    d. Keep cool

12. Not exactly known for his speed on the base paths, Ortiz still managed to scare Twins catcher Joe Mauer into dropping a relay throw that would have pegged Papi at the plate. What animal did Ortiz say Mauer must have feared at that moment?

    a. The big elephant
    b. The charging rhino
    c. A rabid dog
    d. A bucking bronco

13. Which Red Sox pitcher paid the following tribute to Hammerin' Hank Aaron: "I'm mad at Hank for deciding to play one more season. I threw him his last home run

and thought I'd be remembered forever. Now, I'll have to throw him another."?

a. Cal Koonce

b. Sparky Lyle

c. Bill "Spaceman" Lee

d. Jim Lonborg

14. As BoSox manager, feisty Don Zimmer gave players (and the press) an earful and exhorted them to loftier heights. Which of the following elements did "Popeye" NOT claim was a way to make up for a lack of talent?

a. Desire

b. Hustle

c. Giving a hundred and ten percent all the time

d. Eating, sleeping, and dreaming baseball

15. Despite the tough times every manager faces during a long baseball season, Zimmer always looked on the bright side: "The weather's cold. My club's bad. My ____ hurts. I can't putt no more. I'm off my ____. My wife's nagging me. Other than that, everything's great." What words are missing from Zim's classic quote?

a. Knee / diet

b. Head / rocker

c. Back / high horse

d. Whole body / soapbox

16. In spring training, Ben (played by actor Jimmy Fallon) was asked by a reporter how the BoSox ranked in terms of

importance in his life. In which order did he answer in the definitive Red Sox movie, *Fever Pitch*?

    a. "I say breathing… the Red Sox… and sex."

    b. "I say the Red Sox… sex… and breathing."

    c. "I say sex… the Red Sox… and breathing."

17. The Red Sox finally took the cake in 2004 after 86 years of trying. One player stated the following: "You know, a lot of people say they didn't want to die until the Red Sox won the World Series. Well, there could be a lot of busy ambulances tomorrow." Who said it?

    a. Ellis Burks

    b. Kevin Youkilis

    c. Curt Schilling

    d. Johnny Damon

18. American novelist and short story writer John Cheever once wrote: "All literary men are _____ fans—to be a _____ fan in a literate society is to endanger your life." In which order did he list the following two teams?

    a. Red Sox / Yankee

    b. Yankee / Red Sox

19. Red Sox owner Larry Lucchino is credited with the quote: "The New York Yankees are baseball's evil empire, and they're proud of it." What was the real reason behind his famous quip in 2002?

    a. The Yanks took the Red Sox to court for copyright infringement.

    b. The Yanks stole signs from Boston coaches.

c. The Yanks outbid the BoSox for free agent Jose Contreras.

d. The Yanks tried to avoid paying the league's new luxury tax in 1996.

20. After the Red Sox vanquished the Yankees in 2004, Curt Schilling was summoned by David Letterman on his late-night talk show in New York. Which of the following was NOT one of the "Top 10 Secrets" for the Sox blasting the Damn Yankees?

   a. "Unlike the first three games, we didn't leave early to beat the traffic."

   b. "We put flu virus in Jeter's Gatorade."

   c. "It's not like we haven't won a big game before—it's just been 86 years."

   d. "Honestly, I think we were tired of hearing about the Celtics."

QUIZ ANSWERS

1. D – Ted Williams

2. A – True

3. C – Run marathons

4. B – Japan

5. A – Pawtucket, RI

6. C – A phone booth

7. C – His leg, "Because I want to keep my arm in good shape, I need to have my legs in good shape. Without a leg, there is no arm."

8. D – Slider, his dog

9. B – "It's not always going to be roses or flowers."

10. A – A lot of rice and beans

11. C – Swing

12. A – The big elephant

13. C – Bill "Spaceman" Lee

14. D – Eating, sleeping, and dreaming baseball

15. A – Knee / diet

16. B – "I say the Red Sox… sex… and breathing."

17. D – Johnny Damon

18. A – Red Sox / Yankee

19. C – The Yanks outbid the BoSox for free agent Jose Contreras.

20. D – "Honestly, I think we were tired of hearing about the Celtics." (In fact, "the Patriots")

DID YOU KNOW?

1. What do you do when a pro player you look up to just isn't that tall? BoSox slugger Andrew Benintendi picked Dustin Pedroia (also affectionately known as "Little Pedey") as his idol: "Growing up, I was a big Red Sox fan and looked up to guys like Dustin Pedroia who's obviously not the biggest guy, but the way he competes, the way he works, was motivating for me."

2. Not many major cities have the same claim to fame as Boston in one year: "2004 was a great year for Boston! The Patriots won the Super Bowl! Boston hosted its first national political convention! And—the Red Sox won the World Series!" exclaimed Thomas Menino, Boston mayor at the time.

3. Many attempts to describe "Red Sox Nation" have been made, but manager Dick Williams was perhaps the winner: "New York is great, but the New England fans are probably the most knowledgeable and ardent fans, and not just in baseball, but all sports. And Red Sox Nation is Red Sox Nation."

4. Another nickname given to Dustin Pedroia by the Latino players was "El Caballito" or "Little Pony" due to his energy and the belief he could do everything. Big Papi Ortiz always tried to beat Pedroia to the ballpark, but by the time he arrived, Dustin "had already eaten breakfast,

worked out, read the newspaper, played cards, and was ready to play."

5. Asked about his experience catching the wicked knuckler Tim Wakefield let fly in 2004, Jason Varitek quipped, "It's never relaxing, that's for sure. It's like snowflakes—no two are ever alike. Wake's thrown about 3,000 knucklers, and I know I've caught at least one of 'em."

6. The Red Sox 2007 championship season featured two outstanding Japanese pitchers, Daisuke Matsuzaka and Hideki Okajima, who said upon arrival he would be "a hero in the dark" to not overshadow the former star. Teammate Manny Ramírez put it in a nutshell: "Those Japanese guys know how to paint."

7. Not many players terrorized opponent pitchers like Manny Ramírez during his Beantown reign. Manny never shunned the spotlight: "I ain't got no problem in Boston, I especially like the attention. I know that I'm one of the top guys in the game and all the attention is on me. I got a lot of people on my shoulder, but I'm human."

8. The unofficial BoSox anthem, Neil Diamond's "Sweet Caroline," was the favorite of Amy Toby, who picked the tunes played at Fenway from 1998-2004. Diamond himself showed up to sing it for fans after the 2013 Boston Marathon bombing. The lyrics, "Hands, touchin' hands, Reachin' out, touchin' me, touchin' you," brought some relief.

9. Wade Boggs banged out countless hits for the Sox over the

years. And if you ever tinkered with a car, you'll understand Wade's diagnosis of batting: "A swing is like a car. You've got the fan belt, carburetor, pistons, spark plugs, fuel pump. If any part isn't working, the car doesn't run. Same way with hitting."

10. Despite leaving the Sox after 12 years for so-called greener pastures in New York, Roger "Rocket" Clemens's work ethic still endeared him to Boston fans. "I think anything is possible if you have the mindset and the will and desire to do it and put the time in," he asserted.

CHAPTER 4:

RED SOX RECORDS

QUIZ TIME!

1. On April 20, 2012, Guinness World Records ascertained that a new world record was set at Fenway Park to celebrate its centennial year. Almost 40,000 cans of Welch's Sparkling Grape Juice were handed out to thirsty fans for the toast. How many fans were actually there?

    a. 35,710
    b. 35,017
    c. 32,904
    d. 32,409

2. You know that some records aren't meant to be broken. Besides being beaned horrifically on the cheekbone, "Tony C" Conigliaro bashed BoSox and MLB records after signing at age 17. One such record is the youngest player to ever hit 200 homers. How old was Tony at the time?

    a. 20
    b. 21

c. 22

d. 24

3. Dwight Evans was the free-swinging right fielder for Boston for a full 19 years. Considering that he was nominated as one of the nine "best arms" in MLB history, and led the American League with 256 dingers from 1980-1989, what record did he set on Opening Day in 1986?

    a. He took Jack Morris of the Tigers deep on the first pitch of the season.
    b. He homered in his first at-bat for the fourth consecutive year.
    c. He cranked a walk-off homer as the Sox beat the Tigers for the fourth straight year.
    d. He threw out four Tiger runners in a single game.

4. The 2004 Series-winning Sox were dubbed "the idiots," and Johnny Damon was certainly one of them. He also tied a Major League record with three hits in one inning. But Johnny's feat was even more special. In what way?

    a. All his hits were in the ninth inning, and he also scored three runs.
    b. All his hits were triples.
    c. All his hits were in the first inning, including a triple, double, and single.
    d. All his hits were infield hits.

5. This Boston batter was a 1st round draft pick in 1994, elected to six All-Star Games, and won two batting titles. He also broke a Major League record by hitting three

round-trippers in two consecutive innings—on his birthday, no less. Who was he?

   a. Otis "Trot" Nixon

   b. Nomar Garciaparra

   c. Carlos Rodriguez

   d. Ted Williams

6. The BoSox scored Bill Mueller as a free agent in 2003. Best known for his clutch RBI single in the ALCS against Yank ace Mariano Rivera, Mueller also set another record unlikely to be broken. What was it?

   a. He was intentionally walked five straight times in a game.

   b. He had five hits along with five putouts in a single game.

   c. He had four first-pitch hits in one game.

   d. He hit two grand slams, from opposite sides of the plate, in two straight at-bats.

7. Roger "The Rocket" Clemens clinched his place as one of the greatest Boston and MLB pitchers of all time. Clemens is the only hurler in history to have two 20-strikeout games to his credit.

   a. True

   b. False

8. The pundits called Boston's Ted Williams the "greatest pure hitter" ever to play the game. Besides being a 17-time All-Star, winning the Triple Crown and MVP award—

both twice, he also detonated the rookie record for RBIs. How many did he bat in?

a. 105

b. 125

c. 145

d. 165

9. Pedro Martinez sauntered into Beantown in 1997 from the Montreal Expos. He proceeded to put together seven straight brilliant seasons on the mound, especially 2000 (some say simply "the best year ever"). In what category did Pedro lead all of MLB for five seasons overall?

a. Most strikeouts

b. Earned run average (ERA)

c. Highest strikeout-to-walk ratio

d. Least runs scored against

10. Remember how to spell the last name of Carl Yastrzemski? Don't forget it! Yaz won the Triple Crown back in 1967 and was inducted into the MLB Hall of Fame in only his first year eligible. What mark did Yaz reach before any other American League player?

11. 2,800 hits and 2,400 walks

a. The player with his name misspelled more times than any other

b. 3,000 hits and 400 homers

c. 4,000 hits and 500 homers

12. Freddy Lynn patrolled center field for the Sox, starting for six years, making spectacular catches look smooth. He also

was the first MLB player to win the Rookie of the Year, Gold Glove, and MVP in the same season (1975). Who's the only other player to match Lynn?

    a. Barry Bonds

    b. Chipper Jones

    c. Sammy Sosa

    d. Ichiro Suzuki

13. While the Sox went 86 years without a World Series title to their names, they also piled up some playoff losses from 1986-1995—13 consecutive games to be precise. This ignominious record was finally broken when the Minnesota Twins reached 14 in 2019.

    a. True

    b. False

14. The 2003 BoSox bashed many club and MLB records: most extra-base hits by a team in one season (649), most hits in a game (six singles by Nomar Garciaparra), and most men left on base by one player in a single game (12 by Trot Nixon!). What nickname did the team inherit that year?

    a. The Boston Bashers

    b. The Boston Tea Partiers

    c. Cowboy Up Sox

    d. Sox Home on the Range

15. July of 2003 was a particularly hot month—not for the temperature, but the Boston bats. What record did the team set for most homers in a month?

a. 48

b. 55

c. 60

d. 70

16. You may be able to find some spicy food at Fenway, but there were two occasions when real fires laid waste to sections of the venerable stadium. The first time, in 1926, Red Sox owner John Quinn declined to fix the damage. Why?

    a. Lack of funds

    b. Lack of interest

    c. He thought the charred bleachers were more attractive.

    d. Lack of similar wood to rebuild the burned bleachers

17. Fenway's left-field wall, affectionately known as the Green Monster, soars over the outfield and has always been an enticing target for right-handed hitters. There are also as many as 211,000 dents in the wall.

    True

    False

18. Indeed, the Green Monster wasn't painted green until 1947. It was rebuilt of tin once after a fire and is now composed of hard plastic. What was the Monster's original purpose?

    a. To make left-field home runs more difficult

    b. To prevent non-paying fans from watching from the street

c. To prevent the cold sea breeze off Back Bay from affecting the game

d. To block the sun during afternoon games

19. Fans in the know are familiar with the right-field foul pole named after Johnny Pesky. Which famous slugger was the left-field foul pole dedicated to in 2005?

    a. Carlton Fisk
    b. Big Papi Ortiz
    c. Rick Burleson
    d. Jim Rice

20. Just prior to the 1912 season, the Red Sox decided to face a local university team with similar colors. In terrible New England spring weather, the big leaguers prevailed 2-0. Who was the opponent?

    a. Boston College Eagles
    b. MIT Marauders
    c. Northeastern Huskies
    d. Harvard Crimson

21. Next time you attend a game at Fenway (Let's hope it's soon!), you're almost obligated to buy the ubiquitous "Fenway Frank" accompanied by an ice-cold beer. But the draft in Fenway is sure to set you back at $7.75 (And that was in 2016!). Which parks have the cheapest beer in MLB?

    a. Arizona and Cleveland
    b. Milwaukee and Texas
    c. San Francisco and Seattle
    d. Baltimore and Philadelphia

QUIZ ANSWERS

1. C – 32,904

2. C – 22

3. A – He took Jack Morris of the Tigers deep on the first pitch of the season.

4. C – All his hits were in the first inning, including a triple, double, and single.

5. B – Nomar Garciaparra

6. D – He hit two grand slams, from opposite sides of the plate, in two straight at-bats.

7. A – True

8. C – 145

9. B – Earned run average (ERA)

10. C – 3,000 hits and 400 homers

11. D – Ichiro Suzuki

12. A – True

13. C – Cowboy Up Sox

14. B – 55

15. A – Lack of funds

16. A – True, There are up to 211,000 dents according to a *Boston Globe* estimate.

17. B – To prevent non-paying fans from watching from the street

18. A – Carlton Fisk

19. D – Harvard Crimson

20. A – Arizona and Cleveland, About $4

DID YOU KNOW?

1. Once a batting cage for the visitors and storage for the Sox, the Bleacher Bar opened in 2008. The bar sits snugly under the outfield seats at Fenway. While you might be tempted to run onto the field to catch a fly ball with beer in hand, a glass partition separates the bar and grass.

2. The Sox have designated a special red seat in the bleachers where, in 1946, Ted Williams apparently belted a 502-foot homer to break the straw hat of a napping Yankee fan from Albany, Joe Boucher.

3. While the origin of "The Wave" enjoyed by fans the world over will always be disputed, Sox fans claim that when one of their ranks ducked out for a beer, the entire row had to stand up due to the tight space. The row behind also stood to continue watching the game in ever-crowded Fenway.

4. How did that letter "x" get at the end of Sox anyway? The team changed its name from the Boston Americans back in 1907 to the Red Socks, but management didn't like the looks of that long word on their uniforms. So, the Red Sox were born in one of the first "modern" marketing moves by the astute owners.

5. As you surely remember from a previous quiz, there were untold efforts made to banish "the Curse of the Bambino" through the decades. One renowned singer named Jimmy

Buffet made fun of the radical Red Sox fans by "channeling" the Babe in a song.

6. A less humorous note (and a testament to the extremeness of some Sox fans): when Bill Buckner inexplicably let the Mets' Mookie Wilson's weak grounder squirm through his legs in 1986, he received death threats. His manager McNamara had made the decision to leave his questionable glove in the lineup, but the fans let the skipper slide.

7. "Billy Buck" received a measure of forgiveness when the Sox honored their 2007 world champions. Buckner was invited to toss out the ceremonial first pitch together with former teammate Dwight Evans and was greeted by a warm round of applause from the Fenway faithful.

8. Jumping back to 1917, still with the Sox, Babe was ejected by umpire Brick Owens after arguing over a four-pitch walk. Ernie Shore came on in relief after the dustup between Ruth and Owens, and when the runner was quickly caught stealing, then recorded 26 straight outs for a perfect game.

9. Despite the talented Boston pitching staff through the years, including Cy Young, Lefty Grove, and Roger "Rocket" Clemens, it was none other than Smoky Joe Wood who compiled the best-ever ERA of 1.99 for the franchise. Before injury in 1915, Wood quipped about himself: "I threw so hard I thought my arm would fly right off my body."

10. In his final bat in Boston, Ted "The Splendid Splinter"

Williams pulverized his 521st round-tripper. He later admitted that he almost tipped his cap to the Sox faithful in attendance, but he'd decided 20 years earlier to never make such a gesture: "It wasn't because I didn't think the Red Sox fans were the greatest. They were the greatest fans in the world."

CHAPTER 5:

HOW ABOUT A TRADE?

QUIZ TIME!

1. Everybody knows of the blockbuster trade that sent the Babe to New York in 1920. But who actually was Boston's first recorded signing from another team?

   a. Duffy Lewis was discovered in Yuma, AZ, and drafted in 1908.
   b. Aaron Judge was lured from the Yankees in 2017.
   c. Judge Nagle was acquired from the Pirates for cash in 1911.
   d. Cy "Cyclone" Young was enticed to the Boston Americans from St. Louis in 1901.

2. When talking about trades, we can't focus only on players or teams, but sometimes leagues. When the youthful Western League came, challenging the established National League, the Buffalo franchise was cancelled in favor of a Boston team called the Americans.

   a. True
   b. False

3. Before the consummation of the Bambino trade, the Boston Americans already set a precedent by sending a controversial player to the New York Highlanders in 1904. Who was he?

   a. Pat Donoghue
   b. Paddy Dooley
   c. Patsy Dougherty
   d. Pasty Doughboy

4. In 1912, New York Giants outfielder Fred Snodgrass seemed to have traded places with the Sox Bill Buckner some 75 years later. He dropped a fly to let the Sox back in the game, and Boston went on to win the Series. What was his error called?

   a. Snodgrass's Miss
   b. Snodgrass's Muff
   c. Snodgrass Miffed
   d. Snodgrass's Whiff

5. When Red Sox owner Joseph Lannin signed Babe Ruth in 1915, they soon traded away an established star which some say allowed the Babe to blossom. Who was the man sent packing?

   a. Harry Hooper
   b. Duffy Lewis
   c. Smoky Joe Wood
   d. Tris Speaker

6. Harry Frazee, the owner responsible for shipping the Babe, bought the Sox in 1916 for almost a half million

dollars. Before the Babe deal, he engineered another multi-player trade with the Yanks. Which one of these players was NOT involved?

  a. Dutch Leonard
  b. Duffy Lewis
  c. Slim Love
  d. King Bader

7. Frazee also unloaded submarine-style pitching sensation Carl Mays to the Yankees just prior to Ruth in 1919. What kind of problem had Mays posed while in Boston?

  a. Discipline
  b. Drinking
  c. Smoking cigars in the bathroom
  d. Womanizing

8. Shortly before the Big Bambino was traded to the Yankees, he had broken the single-season home run record. How many homers did Ruth swat during that season?

  a. 25
  b. 29
  c. 36
  d. 45

9. Another reason cited at the time for Ruth's straight sale to the Yankees was his myriad disciplinary problems. His Ruthian behavior continued in New York.

  a. True
  b. False

10. After Frazee decided to get out of baseball altogether, he started selling players left and right—especially to the Yanks. In 1921, who were two of these uniquely named players?

    a. Bullet Joe Bush and Sad Sam Jones

    b. Broadway Joe Namath and Matt Snell

    c. George Burns and Sam Dodge

    d. Rip Collins and Jack Quinn

11. Not every player who jumped the Red Sox ship for the Yankees returned to haunt their former club. Alan Embree shut down the Yanks in 2004 but was later released. What was his ERA when New York picked him up?

    a. 5.32

    b. 6.54

    c. 7.65

    d. 9.11

12. After being drafted and developed wholly by the Red Sox, Jacoby Ellsbury helped the Boston boys to two World Series rings. He then signed which monster deal with the Yankees?

    a. 3 years for $66 million

    b. 5 years for $105 million

    c. 7 years for $153 million

    d. 8 years for $160 million

13. Luis Tiant was a Red Sox star in 1972 after initially playing with the Cleveland Indians and Minnesota Twins. He then left the Red Sox for the Yankees, of all teams. Now retired,

you can often find him outside Fenway. What does he do there?

    a. He flips burgers at his concession stand.

    b. He serves popcorn at his concession stand.

    c. He helps his brother build concession stands.

    d. He signs autographs outside his concession stand.

14. After Wade Boggs spent 11 years with the Sox, he also headed to the Yankees where he won the World Series in 1996. What reason did he give for migrating south to New York?

    a. The Red Sox didn't allow him to pitch.

    b. The sudden death of Sox owner Jean Yawkey caused his contract to be pulled.

    c. The sudden arrival of another third baseman made him nervous.

    d. The Red Sox told him he would play only one more year as a starter.

15. Although Roger Clemens later ended up with the Yankees, which team did he first flee to while spurning the Red Sox?

    a. Chicago White Sox

    b. Colorado Rockies

    c. Toronto Blue Jays

    d. San Diego Padres

16. Before splitting Beantown for top dollar from the Yanks in 2005, Johnny Damon said the following: "It's definitely not the most important thing to go out there for the top dollar,

which the Yankees are going to offer me. It's not what I need."?

a. True
b. False

17. Kevin Youkilis was instrumental in helping Boston win the Series in 2007. When he would apparently be traded to the ChiSox, he left Fenway to a rousing ovation. Which team did he actually sign with?

a. Arizona Diamondbacks
b. Miami Marlins
c. New York Mets
d. New York Yankees

18. Carl Mays was so fed up in with the lack of run production in Boston in 1919 that he demanded a trade to the Yankees. What tragic record is Mays associated with?

a. He's the only player to have a losing record with all six teams he played with.
b. He's the only player in MLB history to accidentally kill an opposing player with a pitch.
c. He's the only player in MLB history to have married and divorced his manager's daughter.
d. He's the only player to have more parking tickets than wins in his final season.

19. After managing Boston for three years and winning a ring, Ed Barrow bolted for the Yankees where he managed from 1921 to 1945. How many rings did he bring home during that time?

a. 2

b. 5

c. 7

d. 10

20. It's claimed that Johnny Damon played better for the Yankees than the Red Sox after his trade, even though he was older. Why?

    a. The short right-field fence was perfect for a left-handed batter like Damon.

    b. The Yankee pinstripes made him look thinner, resulting in more paid endorsements.

    c. The weather in New York was more appropriate for his base-stealing efforts.

    d. He shaved his beard in New York and played like a much younger man.

QUIZ ANSWERS

1. D – Cy "Cyclone" Young was enticed to the Boston Americans from St. Louis in 1901.

2. A – True

3. C – Patsy Dougherty

4. B – Snodgrass's Muff

5. D – Tris Speaker

6. D – King Bader

7. A – Discipline

8. B – 29

9. A – True

10. A – Bullet Joe Bush and Sad Sam Jones

11. C – 7.65

12. C – 7 years for $153 million

13. D – He signs autographs outside his concession stand.

14. B – The sudden death of Sox owner Jean Yawkey caused his contract to be pulled.

15. C – Toronto Blue Jays

16. A – True

17. D – New York Yankees

18. B – He's the only player in MLB history to accidentally kill an opposing player with a pitch.

19. D – 10

20. A – The short right-field fence was perfect for a left-handed batter like Damon.

DID YOU KNOW?

1. For every fan who trades playing cards, there are obviously two that fetch the highest value. But they don't include Babe Ruth as you might imagine, as the Bambino is more associated with New York. The Ted Williams and Carl "Yaz" Yastrzemski cards bring the most cash and interest.

2. If you ever happen upon a Honus Wagner card, don't let it go! You may be sitting on a cool $3.12 million. That's because the Pirates' Honus made the American Tobacco Company stop the release of his card: at most, only 200 were released. A 1916 Babe card can net you about $700K.

3. Babe's card brings big bucks, as well as his bat (the one he used to swat his first dinger as a Yank), which is worth $1.3 million. Wouldn't you know: the contract sending Ruth from the Sox to the Yanks (the most infamous transaction in hardball history?) made $996K in a 2005 auction.

4. Ted Williams's autograph was intensely marketed in the 1980s and early '90s while "Teddy Ballgame" was a steady feature on the sports memorabilia show circuit. Only in 1994, when Ted suffered the first of his two strokes, did his signature fall in value.

5. BoSox fans remained angry about the Babe sale for some 86 years. More recently, Boston fans went berserk after Mookie Betts was dealt to the Dodgers. Why? Mookie's

meteoric rise from rookie to superstar happened right in front of the Fenway faithful. A 2018 ring didn't hurt either.

6. In 1997, Boston made a big move to finally offset the loss of Clemens by bringing in one Pedro Martinez from the Expos. Pedro's BoSox career culminated in his Game 3 gem to corral the Cardinals in 2004. Who was Pedro traded for? Two "prospects": Carl Pavano and Tony Armas Jr.

7. Slightly before Pedro arrived, BoSox GM Dan Duquette took advantage of Seattle's situation to grab Jason Varitek, who became the starting catcher, and Derek Lowe, a starter and closer on the almighty 2004 and 2007 teams. Seattle got Heathcliff Slocumb who plummeted with the Ms.

8. In 2003, GM Theo Epstein spent his whole Thanksgiving holiday trying to sign Curt Schilling away from Arizona. The deal went down to the wire, and the Big Schill finally waived his no-trade clause. You know the rest.

9. When Chris Sale changed his "sox" in 2016, Dave Dombrowski, president of baseball ops, persuaded him to leave the Windy City for a home in Boston. He soon recorded 300 strikeouts in a season and strode out of the pen in 2018 for the final out in Dodgers Stadium. Sox win!

10. When the Sox wrangled Josh Beckett from the Miami Marlins in 2005, third baseman Mike Lowell was "a throw-in" after his previous disastrous season at the plate. Lowell however had other ideas as he resurrected his bat and became the 2007 Series MVP.

CHAPTER 6:

CHAT ABOUT STATS

QUIZ TIME!

1. Who is the Red Sox all-time leader in home runs, with 521?

    a. Jim Rice
    b. Carl Yastrzemski
    c. Big Papi Ortiz
    d. Ted Williams

2. The youngest ever general manager in MLB history was Theo Epstein, hired by the Sox in 2002. Theo was instrumental in Boston's first ring in eight decades in 2004. How old was he upon hiring?

    a. 26
    b. 28
    c. 30
    d. 34

3. Amazingly, after only nine years and two Series rings, Epstein resigned from Boston and went to the Chicago Cubs where he helped the team to its first World Series

win in a long spell. How many years was it since the Cubbies had last won?

    a. 96 years

    b. 100 years

    c. 108 years

    d. 115 years

4. Luis Tiant dazzled on the Sox mound in 1968. And it wasn't such a good idea to try to steal a base against "El Tiante" either. How many tried and how many were caught that year?

    a. 9 steal attempts / 9 caught

    b. 15 steal attempts / 13 caught

    c. 21 steal attempts / 20 caught

5. From 1957-1968 with Boston, Cleveland, and Minnesota, Russ Nixon was not known as fabulously fleet of foot. In fact, the catcher played in 2,504 games in his career without stealing a single base (even Big Papi had 11 stolen bags in his career!).

    a. True

    b. False

6. Rickey Henderson set the MLB record for stolen bases. In addition, "the Man of Steal" was caught trying to run 335 times. At what age did he become the oldest MLB star to enter a game?

    a. 39

    b. 41

c. 43

d. 46

7. Herman Long didn't actually play for the Americans or Red Sox, but rather for the Boston Beaneaters from 1890 to 1902. He shattered the MLB record with 1,096 in which category?

   a. Most career assists

   b. Most career errors

   c. Most men left on base (LOB) in a season

   d. Most career putouts

8. In 2018, Chris Sale recorded the first and last outs in the World Series for the first time since Hal Newhouser in 1945. How many other players have accomplished the same feat?

   a. 2

   b. 4

   c. 6

   d. 8

9. When David Price and the BoSox pitching staff retired 16 straight Dodger batters in Game 6 of the 2018 Series, it was the longest streak since Don Larsen in 1956. What is Larsen best known for?

   a. Pitching a perfect game

   b. Winning the most games ever in a single season

   c. Finishing a season with zero losses

   d. Driving a classic car

10. Steve Pearce punished Dodger pitchers in the 2018 Series with three dingers—in all of 24 hours. Whose Red Sox record did he equal for World Series homers?

    a. Wade Boggs
    b. Dwight Evans
    c. Big Papi Ortiz
    d. Manny Ramírez

11. The aforementioned Pearce's multi-homer performance in a Series-clinching game placed him in rare company. Which of the following players did NOT do the same?

    a. Johnny Bench
    b. Kirk Gibson
    c. Duke Snider
    d. Aaron Boone

12. Boston's Ted Williams worked magic with his bat, and his career on-base percentage (OBP) of .482 has never been equaled. What is Williams regarded as?

    a. The greatest hitter of all time
    b. The greatest fielder of all time
    c. The best base runner of all time
    d. The best all-around player of all time

13. Boston pitcher Cy Young's arm surely must have been elastic. Even though he pitched before the modern era, he reveled in 511 wins. How many complete games did he have?

    a. 650
    b. 701

c. 749

d. 776

14. If you carefully check the record books, you won't find this feat. But the 2004 BoSox climbed out of a 3-0 hole in the ALCS against the Yanks, and then swept the Cards in the Series for an eight-game winning streak.

    a. True
    b. False

15. In the so-called "dead-ball era," Detroit's Ty Cobb had the highest career batting average of .367. In the "live-ball era," Ted Williams was the man. What was his career BA?

    a. .339
    b. .344
    c. .355
    d. .366

16. Though Mike Cameron didn't catapult the ball for the BoSox like he did for his other clubs, he's one of the only hitters in MLB history to bash four homers in one game. Mike's also a member of the "250/250 club." What do those numbers represent?

    a. 250 doubles / 250 triples
    b. 250 homers / 250 stolen bases
    c. 250 homers / 250 triples
    d. 250 strikeouts / 250 walks in the same season

17. The most career home runs by an American League pitcher was 37 by Wes Farrell, mostly in the 1930s. What other teams did he play for besides Boston?

a. Baltimore, Texas, and Toronto
b. Cleveland, New York, and Washington
c. Chicago, New York, and Atlanta
d. Baltimore, Philadelphia, and Charlotte

18. The illustrious Tris Speaker battered the all-time MLB record of most outfield assists, with 449. What was the main reason given for Speaker's success?

    a. He played an extremely shallow center field.
    b. He had blazing speed, allowing him to reach any ball.
    c. His vision tested as better than any other Boston player ever.
    d. The glove he wore was considerably smaller than other outfielders.

19. Despite losing the 1967 Fall Classic, the Red Sox set a record for hammering three homers in the same inning. Which of these players did NOT crush one?

    a. Carl Yastrzemski
    b. José Tartabull
    c. Rico Petrocelli
    d. Reggie Smith

20. Some say that baseball's a bit slow. The extra-inning affair between the Pawtucket Red Sox and Rochester Red Wings (Triple A) took 8 hours and 25 minutes, stretching over 33 innings of play.

    a. True
    b. False

QUIZ ANSWERS

1. D – Ted Williams

2. B – 28

3. C – 108 years

4. A – 9 steal attempts / 9 caught

5. A – True

6. C – 43

7. B – Most career errors

8. D – 8

9. A – Pitching a perfect game

10. C – Big Papi Ortiz

11. D – Aaron Boone

12. A – The greatest hitter of all time

13. C – 749

14. A – True

15. B – .344

16. B – 250 homers / 250 stolen bases

17. B – Cleveland, New York, and Washington

18. A – He played an extremely shallow center field.

19. B – José Tartabull

20. A – True

DID YOU KNOW?

1. The 2018 version of the Sox didn't lose four straight games at any point during the season. The only other teams to achieve that high-flying mark in franchise history were the 1903 and 2003 squads, both of which also won the Series.

2. Many don't miss Wade Boggs in Boston (after his dubious decision to join the Yanks). But there's no doubt about his batting: he had two seasons with at least 150 singles, 50 extra-base hits, and 100 walks. Nobody had even one monster season like that. He and Pete Rose are the only players in baseball history with even 150 singles, 50 extra-base hits, and 75 walks in multiple seasons (four and three for the two players respectively).

3. Only for your information, Wade Boggs also holds a world record with the International Game Fish Association for the largest bluefish ever caught at 87 centimeters.

4. You may ask why Boggs was ever foolish enough to leave the cozy confines of Fenway. He hit for a .369 average there, blasting mostly singles in the storied park. That average (at home) was eight points higher than Ted Williams's.

5. Boston's brilliant history stretches back practically 120 years, but the team has only retired the numbers of 20 players, starting with Bobby Doerr (#1) and Joe Cronin (#4) and bringing us up to date with Jason Varitek (#33) and Tim Wakefield (#49).

6. Following in the footsteps of Ted and Yaz, Jim Rice manned left field for the Sox for years. Although he was an awesome hitter in his prime, the Baseball Writers Association of America (BBWAA) forced him to wait till his 15th and final year of eligibility in 2009 to elect him to the Hall of Fame.

7. Harry Hooper must at least receive honorable mention for a retired number as he spent 12 of 17 Hall of Fame seasons with the Red Sox. Hooper's problem was that he stopped playing in 1920, a full decade before the uniforms had numbers.

8. We keep coming back to Fenway Park (and hope we always do!). Another Fenway curiosity is the stadium's capacity: 37,305 fans can squeeze in for day games, and 37,775 at night.

9. Fenway celebrated its 500th consecutive sellout game on July 19, 2009. The venerable Boston franchise joined two NBA teams who managed 500 or more sellouts: The Dallas Mavericks and Portland Trailblazers.

10. Due to its odd shape and traditional hand-operated scoreboard, Fenway also has some funky rules: "A ball going through the scoreboard, either on the bounce or fly, is a ground rule double."

CHAPTER 7:

DRAFT DAY

QUIZ TIME!

1. Since the First-Year Player Draft system was established in the Majors, the Red Sox have drafted 70 1st round choices. How many were pitchers?

    a. 15

    b. 24

    c. 31

    d. 45

2. Which of the following states did NOT provide the bulk of players that Boston drafted?

    a. California

    b. Connecticut

    c. South Carolina

    d. Texas

3. Two of Boston's 1st round picks have gone on to garner World Series rings. Who are they?

    a. Maurice "Mo" Vaughan and Sam Horn

    b. Craig Hansen and Taylor Hanson

c. Daniel Bard and Richard Nixon

d. Jacoby Ellsbury and Trot Nixon

4. Maurice Samuel "Mo" Vaughan, drafted by the Red Sox in 1989, had another nice nickname. What was it?

   a. The Hit Man

   b. The Hit Dog

   c. Mo for Your Money

   d. The Hit Parade

5. Sam Horn came to the Sox as the 16th pick in the 1982 Draft. What dubious hitting achievement is Horn best known for (though seven others have matched his performance)?

   a. He was hit by a pitch in five consecutive games.

   b. He struck out six times in a single game.

   c. He left his glove at home before a critical game.

   d. He struck out twice in the same inning.

6. Two other records belong to Boston draftee Sam Horn. As a member of the Orioles, he scored his first run ever to inaugurate Baltimore's new stadium, Camden Yards, and he was the highest paid foreign player in the history of Taiwan ($216K in 1997).

   a. True

   b. False

7. Ace pitcher Clay Buchholz was drafted by Boston in 2005 and threw a no-hitter in only his second start as a Major Leaguer. How many other Sox hurlers have thrown no-hitters?

a. 10

b. 13

c. 16

d. 22

8. Who is the only BoSox 1st rounder to make it all the way to the Hall of Fame?

a. Nomar Garciaparra

b. Jim Rice

c. Reymond Fuentes

d. Wilson Álvarez

9. At the time that the First-Year Player Draft system was instituted in 1965, compensatory picks were also allowed. What were these picks for?

a. For when a team fails to finish in the top five teams of its division in two straight years

b. For when a team's attendance falls by 40% or more compared to the prior year

c. For when a team's performance is at least 25% worse than the previous year

d. For when a team loses an especially valuable free agent in the previous off-season

10. Which 1st round draft pick did the Red Sox fail to sign in 1970?

a. Danny Mack

b. Jimmy Hack

c. Greg McMurtry

d. Bob Zupcic

11. Boston drafted Roger Clemens in 1983 from the University of Texas, and he went on to win three Cy Young Awards and an MVP Award with the Sox. With which of the following teams did he NOT win the Cy Young?

   a. Chicago White Sox
   b. Houston Astros
   c. New York Yankees
   d. Toronto Blue Jays

12. The 1994 Draft brought Nomar Garciaparra to Boston from the Georgia Institute of Technology. What award did he win a scant three years later?

   a. The Triple Crown (given to a player who leads the league in three statistical categories)
   b. The Most Valuable Player
   c. The Rookie of the Year
   d. The Home Run Title

13. Garciaparra was honored with his father's first name, Ramon, spelled backwards. What did his father do to accelerate his baseball development at age 13?

   a. His dad pitted him against a Division 1 pitcher who threw 90 mph.
   b. His dad made him hit bucket after bucket of balls from a pitching machine.
   c. His dad made him run countless laps with ankle weights.
   d. His dad made him take batting practice wearing a blindfold.

14. Christopher Trotman "Trot" Nixon was the Sox top pick in the 1993 Draft and came to embody the hard-working ethic of the "Boston Dirt Dogs" who won the 2004 Series. However, he only received a single vote point for Rookie of the Year. Who won the award that year (1999)?

    a. Freddy Garcia

    b. Tim Hudson

    c. Carlos Beltrán

    d. Billy Koch

15. Shaq Thompson was a top football and baseball prospect, drafted by Boston in 2012. What made him decide to hang up his cleats and focus on football?

    a. He was convinced he would spend too much time in the minors.

    b. He was offered far more money to play football than baseball.

    c. He was picked off first base as a runner in four straight minor league games.

    d. He went 0 for 39 with 37 strikeouts in the Gulf Coast League.

16. After the BoSox were investigated by MLB for sign-stealing during their 2018 campaign, what was part of their punishment?

    a. They were denied a 2nd round draft pick.

    b. They were fined $5 million like the Astros in 2017.

    c. They were stripped of two 1st round picks in 2020 and 2021.

    d. They were given a slap on the wrist.

17. Jackie Bradley Jr. came to the Sox as the 40th pick in the 2011 Draft and played a part in the victorious 2018 campaign. Which school did he start for in the College World Series?

    a. Washington

    b. Nebraska

    c. North Carolina

    d. South Carolina

18. In 2004, the Sox nabbed Dustin Pedroia in the 2nd round from Arizona State University. Besides two World Series titles, what other prestigious individual award has he won three times?

    a. MVP of the American League

    b. The Gold Glove Award

    c. AL Rookie of the Year

    d. Named as Best Interviewee by various Boston radio stations

19. The Sox snagged Mookie Betts with a sweet $750K signing bonus in the 5th round in 2011. What other sport did Betts star in as a teen in Tennessee?

    a. Badminton

    b. Bowling

    c. Kayaking

    d. Lacrosse

20. Pundits say that no team has drafted better than the Red Sox over the years. How many times have the BoSox actually owned a top ten pick?

a. 20
b. 12
c. 8
d. 6

QUIZ ANSWERS

1. C – 31

2. B – Connecticut

3. D – Jacoby Ellsbury and Trot Nixon

4. B – The Hit Dog

5. B – He struck out six times in a single game.

6. A – True

7. C – 16

8. B – Jim Rice

9. D – For when a team loses an especially valuable free agent in the previous off-season

10. B – Jimmy Hack

11. A – Chicago White Sox

12. C – The Rookie of the Year

13. A – His dad pitted him against a Division 1 pitcher who threw 90 mph.

14. C – Carlos Beltrán

15. D – He went 0 for 39 with 37 strikeouts in the Gulf Coast League.

16. A – They were denied a 2nd round draft pick.

17. D – South Carolina

18. B – The Gold Glove Award

19. B – Bowling

20. D – 6

DID YOU KNOW?

1. Bill Lee turned up in the 22nd round of the draft in 1968. Yet, he went on to record 94 wins for the Sox (and 119 in his career) as a soft-throwing left-hander. He also won the nickname "Spaceman" for his odd behavior and hilarious interviews.

2. Mark Teixeira turned down Boston as a high schooler from Maryland, opting instead to attend Georgia Tech (and leaving a $1.5 million signing bonus on the table). He stepped on Red Sox toes again later when he went with the Yanks in 2009.

3. The Red Sox had some draft busts over the years as well. Kris Johnson was highly touted for the 1st round back in 2006. But his lack of an effective "third pitch" never allowed him to progress further than Triple-A Pawtucket.

4. Caleb Clay dominated as a high schooler in Alabama, leading Boston to claim him with the 44th pick in the 2006 Draft. But a Tommy John surgery (using a ligament from another part of the body to repair an arm ligament) took away his power, and he later hit the bottom of the barrel with Double-A Portland.

5. Where do the draft picks usually go before they get the chance to swing for the Green Monster? Commonly known as farm teams, feeder teams, or nursery clubs, places like Triple-A Pawtucket in Rhode Island, Single-A

Greenville Drive in South Carolina, and even two Dominican Summer League Red Sox squads keep the picks busy before the big time.

6. The traditional June draft started in 1965. The old draft occurred in January and yielded some Red Sox gems like Carlton Fisk, Curt Schilling, and Ellis Burks. But that system shut down in 1986.

7. Mike Greenwell was a 3rd round pick in 1982. He spent 12 solid years with Boston, belting the ball this way and that. Greenwell is probably best known for finishing runner-up in the 1988 MVP race to a suspiciously bulked (and juiced) up José Canseco in Oakland.

8. Ben Oglivie was a high pick for the Sox in 1968, but his bat went quiet for most of his three seasons in Beantown. After landing with the Milwaukee Brewers, his bat sprang to life, and he became a key part of the team affectionately called "Harvey's Wallbangers," together with Cecil Cooper, another BoSox draftee.

9. The challenge for some players is that there are only nine positions on a ball team, and sometimes the man ahead of you won't budge. In this case, it was Carlton "Pudge" Fisk who wouldn't let draftee Ernie Whitt get a whiff of the catching action. Ernie was picked up by Toronto in the 1976 Expansion Draft, and he carved out a respectable career north of the border.

10. David Eckstein was the 581st overall pick in 1997, and at only 5 feet 6 inches with a weird swing, didn't look like

he'd make it. Then the Sox started to tinker with his batting style, and he got even worse. In the end, he went back to what worked and won a World Series—with the Cardinals!

CHAPTER 8:

PITCHER & CATCHER TIDBITS

QUIZ TIME!

1. Most fans know of Babe Ruth's slugging exploits, like his career 714 homers (a record only broken by Hammerin' Hank Aaron and Barry Bonds). But Babe was one of the best pitchers ever. What was his career ERA?

    a. 1.993

    b. 2.155

    c. 2.277

    d. 2.865

2. As a pitcher, Ruth was also tough to take long (though, admittedly it was "the dead-ball era"). How many homers did he give up in 1,221 games?

    a. 10

    b. 18

    c. 25

    d. 35

3. The Great Bambino also pitched nine shutouts for Boston in 1916, a record which held up until 1979. Who tied it?

a. Kent Tekulve, Pittsburgh Pirates

b. J.R. Richard, Houston Astros

c. Ron Guidry, New York Yankees

d. Joe Niekro, Atlanta Braves

4. Cy Young's primary team is listed as the Cleveland Spiders, but he powered Boston as a pitcher as well. How many times did he win more than 30 games in a season?

    a. 9

    b. 7

    c. 5

    d. 2

5. On May 5, 1904, Cy Young hurled the Red Sox to victory and, in the process, recorded the first perfect game in AL history, and of the twentieth century. Who was the hapless opponent?

    a. Cleveland Blues

    b. New York Highlanders

    c. Philadelphia Athletics

    d. St. Louis Browns

6. Winning the World Series isn't the only measure of success in MLB. When the BoSox won their first AL pennant in 21 years in 1967, who was the pitching leader of the "Impossible Dream" team?

    a. Elston Howard

    b. Jim Lonborg

    c. Ken Harrelson

    d. Rico Petrocelli

7. Sparky Lyle came on as the reliable Red Sox closer during the "Impossible Dream" season. Ted Williams once told him that one pitch was baseball's best because he couldn't hit it, even though he knew it was coming. What was the pitch?

   a. A slider
   b. A curveball
   c. A knuckler
   d. A two-seam fastball

8. That 1967 team shocked New England by advancing all the way to the Series against the Cards. However, starting catcher Mike Ryan couldn't get the job done, and neither could second-stringer Elston Howard. What was the third-stringer's name who stepped in?

   a. Tony Conigliaro
   b. Russ Gibson
   c. George Scott
   d. José Tartabull

9. As you're aware, the 1986 Sox allowed the Mets back into the Series in inexplicable fashion. Who would've probably been the MVP for the Sox with his two wins and no-decision in Game 7?

   a. Roger Clemens
   b. Bruce Hurst
   c. Al Nipper
   d. Calvin Schiraldi

10. Your catcher or "backstopper" should be able to catch and hit the cover off the ball, two things Carlton Fisk did well. What's Fisk most famous for?

    a. He fought back from injury many times, setting an example for his team.
    b. He worked tirelessly as a catcher and in the community helping the poor.
    c. "The Commander" commanded the BoSox to a record number of wins in 1975.
    d. The homer he "waved fair" beat the Cincinnati Reds in Game 6 of the '75 Series.

11. Fisk still holds the AL record for most years operating behind the plate. How many years did he command the position?

    a. 16
    b. 19
    c. 24
    d. 27

12. Bob Stanley (1977-1989), sinkerball specialist, leads the Red Sox in games pitched (637) and saves (132). On top of that, he's a native New Englander. What state does Bob hail from?

    a. Connecticut
    b. Massachusetts
    c. Maine
    d. Vermont

13. Josh Becket blasted the ball over the plate and helped Boston win it all in 2007. What other team did Josh win the World Series with in 2003?

    a. Florida Marlins
    b. Minnesota Twins
    c. Tampa Bay Rays
    d. Colorado Rockies

14. Derek Lowe was originally a closer until becoming a full-time starter in the Sox 2003 season. While Boston was on its merry way to winning the 2004 Series, what record did D-Lowe set?

    a. He became the youngest pitcher to ever win the MVP.
    b. He became the first pitcher to ever win the clinching game of three playoff series.
    c. He became the first pitcher to ever win two games each in three playoff series.
    d. He became the first pitcher to have a last name that meant the same as his ERA.

15. Tex Hughson (1941-1949), flame-throwing Texan, played for the Sox his entire career. Why did he miss all of the 1945 season?

    a. To recover from a torn elbow ligament
    b. To serve in the military
    c. To care for his sick mother
    d. To take time off to study for a Master's degree

16. Dutch Leonard was allowed to continue throwing his

"spitter" after 1920—along with 25 other pitchers—even though the league had banned spitballs.

a. True
b. False

17. Closing great Jonathan Papelbon ranks 1st in saves in Red Sox history. What was the name of the award he won in 2007?

a. The Delivery Man Award
b. The Best Man Award
c. The Classic Closer Award
d. The Relief Man Award

18. Luis Tiant joined the Red Sox pitching corps on a minor league contract in 1970 at age 30. At that time, what injury was he recovering from?

a. A fractured right collar bone
b. A fractured right fibula
c. A fractured right tibia
d. A fractured right scapula

19. After being traded to the BoSox, Lefty Grove went on to become an All-Star in five of his eight seasons. How old was he when he arrived in Beantown?

a. 29
b. 32
c. 34
d. 37

20. Pedro Martinez's pitching brilliance in 1999 and 2000 is renowned not only due to his shiny stats, but also the so-called "Steroids Era" he played in.

    a. True
    b. False

QUIZ ANSWERS

1. C – 2.277

2. A – 10

3. C – Ron Guidry, New York Yankees

4. C – 5

5. C – Philadelphia Athletics

6. B – Jim Lonborg

7. A – A slider

8. B – Russ Gibson

9. B – Bruce Hurst

10. D – The homer he "waved fair" beat the Cincinnati Reds in Game 6 of the '75 Series.

11. C – 24

12. C – Maine

13. A – Florida Marlins

14. B – He became the first pitcher to ever win the clinching game of three playoff series.

15. B – To serve in the military

16. B – False, He was allowed to continue throwing his "spitter" along with 16 others.

17. A – The Delivery Man Award

18. D – A fractured right scapula, The shoulder bone

19. C – 34

20. A – True

DID YOU KNOW?

1. Pitcher Pedro Martinez also has the second lowest WHIP in Red Sox history. What on earth is that? Walks and Hits per Inning Pitched (WHIP) is a modern measure of pitching effectiveness.

2. Two catchers who were also switch-hitters faced each other directly 122 times in the heated Boston-New York rivalry. Jason Varitek and Jorge Posada have eight All-Star Games and six World Series rings between the two of them.

3. Only two years after finding out he had lymphoma, BoSox left-hander Jon Lester won Game 7 of the World Series over the Colorado Rockies. He then twirled a no-hitter against the Kansas City Royals in May 2008. He was honored for his comeback from the disease with the Tony Conigliaro Award in 2007.

4. Jason Varitek was the Sox captain and helped keep some of the players called "the idiots" in line during their 2004 championship run. But his true challenge was catching Wake's knuckler: "Catching the knuckleball is like catching a fly with chopsticks."

5. On the other hand, the author of 186 team wins for the Sox, Tim Wakefield clearly expressed the difficulties that a knuckleball pitcher faces at times, especially when the ball refuses to flutter. "It's hard to get guys out when you have nothing to get them out with," he quipped.

6. Nicknamed "Rough," Bill Carrigan caught for the Red Sox back in 1906. He was also called "the greatest manager I ever played for" by none other than George Herman "Babe" Ruth Jr.

7. Catcher Rich Gedman had a solid decade behind the plate in Boston from 1980-1990. But he's arguably most famous for controlling the Pawtucket pitchers in that record-breaking 33-inning game. How was that on the knees?

8. Backstopper Rick Ferrell played 18 seasons for Boston and threw out 59% of potential base robbers in 1937. He also served as the battery mate of his brother, Wes, winning a combined 62 games.

9. No Boston-New York argument would be complete without comparing catching rivals Carlton Fisk and Thurman Munson. Forget other stats: Fisk wins hands down in terms of longevity with 21 full seasons to Munson's 10 (cut short by injury).

10. Although Fisk and Munson often appeared to go to war for at least a decade on the diamond, Thurman gets the nod with his WAR (wins above replacement) stat of 3.9 over an average season to Fisk's 2.9. If you love baseball, you gotta love stats!

CHAPTER 9:

ODDS & ENDS

QUIZ TIME!

1. Which of the following songs is NOT played after a BoSox win at Fenway Park?

    a. "Bad to the Bone"

    b. "Dirty Water"

    c. "Joy to the World"

    d. "Tessie"

2. The original "Tessie" song, from the Broadway musical *The Silver Slipper*, is said to have helped the Boston Americans win the World Series in 1903.

    a. True

    b. False

3. The estimated value by Forbes of the Boston Red Sox franchise in 2018 put them in fifth place in MLB. What was the value at the start of the season?

    a. $288 million

    b. $1.65 billion

c. $2.8 billion

d. $1.8 trillion

4. What was the average ticket price for a prized seat at Fenway during the 2017 season?

   a. $44

   b. $56

   c. $29

   d. $38

5. When the Boston Americans became the Red Sox in 1908, what was their average attendance per game at the Huntington Avenue Baseball Grounds?

   a. 3,547

   b. 6,104

   c. 8,734

   d. 11,321

6. When the Red Sox won their "historic" 2004 World Series championship, their total payroll was more than $150 million.

   a. True

   b. False

7. The official BoSox beer is said to be Samuel Adams, named after a legendary Bostonian. Who exactly was this man, born in 1722?

   a. One of America's Founding Fathers who also worked in his father's "malt house"

   b. One of the first men at Harvard in Boston to attempt to play baseball

c. A revolutionary British leader who developed a taste for American beer

d. One of the original patriots to arrive in America aboard the Mayflower

8. Which of the following food items can you NOT find inside Fenway Park?

    a. Brown sugar-glazed bacon on a stick

    b. A lobster roll

    c. A "slammin' onion"

    d. A pizza covered with salmon eggs

9. Fenway Station happens to be a light rail stop on the MBTA Green Line "D" Branch in the Fenway-Kenmore neighborhood. What does MBTA stand for?

    a. Massachusetts Bad Transit Authority

    b. Massachusetts Bay Traffickers Anonymous

    c. Massachusetts Bay Transportation Authority

    d. Massachusetts Bay Transportation Association

10. The Red Sox represent a five-state area called New England in the northeastern part of the United States. Which state is NOT included in this lovely region?

    a. Connecticut

    b. New Hampshire

    c. New Jersey

    d. Vermont

11. In the Red Sox 2019 Media Guide, Jackie Bradley Jr. mentioned he is a distant relative of a particular NBA legend. Who?

a. Larry Bird

b. Magic Johnson

c. Michael Jordan

d. Danny Ainge

12. Of the 43 replay challenges requested of umpires by BoSox manager Alex Cora during the 2018 season, how many were overturned?

a. 15

b. All but one

c. 22

d. 28

13. No player whose last name begins with the letter "X" has ever suited up for Boston.

a. True

b. False

14. Since 2011, current BoSox hurler Nathan Eovaldi has the fastest pitch of all Major Leaguers with 850 or more innings under their belts. What was his velocity?

a. 92.8 mph

b. 94 mph

c. 96.9 mph

d. 99.9 mph

15. Both the Babe and Cy Young before him played in the so-called "dead-ball era." What reason below is one NOT given to explain why this glorious period of hardball has that name?

a. The ball was considered "dead" both by design and overuse.

b. The games were typically low-scoring affairs.

c. The players like Babe were fat and appeared almost dead.

d. Ball-scuffing and adulteration by pitchers was tolerated then.

16. Marty Barrett and Johnny Pesky are the only BoSox players to attempt the "hidden ball play" more than once (each tried the trick three times).

a. True

b. False

17. On June 13, 1989, Red Sox pitcher John Dopson tied the MLB record for most "balks" in a game. How many times did he balk on that fateful day against the Detroit Tigers?

a. 4

b. 6

c. 8

18. Before 2005, the Red Sox managed to play in the postseason more than three seasons in a row.

a. True

b. False

19. It's a long-standing tradition in MLB for visiting players to participate in a specific activity inside the Green Monster wall the first time they ever visit Fenway. What do they normally do?

a. They sign an autograph book placed there.

b. They use the special toilet facility located there.

c. They have a quick cup of coffee with the official scorekeepers.

d. They sign their names on the inside of the wall.

20. From 1912-1933, there was a 10-foot incline sloping up to the wall in left field at Fenway Park. How did this incline become known as "Duffy's Cliff"?

    a. Outfielder Duffy Lewis used to sprint up the incline to catch fly balls.

    b. Outfielder Duffy Lewis was the player who sprained his ankle the most on the incline.

    c. Singer Jerry Lee Lewis was featured in many live shows there.

    d. Outfielder Duffy Cliff wrote a book about his experience there..

QUIZ ANSWERS

1. A – "Bad to the Bone"

2. A – True

3. C – $2.8 billion

4. B – $56

5. B – 6,104

6. B – False, The 2004 payroll was $127,298,500.

7. A – One of America's Founding Fathers who also worked in his father's "malt house"

8. D – A pizza covered with salmon eggs (at least the last time we checked!)

9. C – Massachusetts Bay Transportation Authority

10. C – New Jersey

11. C – Michael Jordan

12. C – 22

13. A – True

14. C – 96.9 mph

15. C – The players like Babe were fat and appeared almost dead.

16. A – True

17. A – 4

18. B – False, After 2005, they've done it three times.

19. D – They sign their names on the inside of the wall.

20. A – Outfielder Duffy Lewis used to sprint up the incline to catch fly balls.

DID YOU KNOW?

1. The Yawkey couple, Thomas and Jean, Boston owners for almost 60 years, decided to memorialize themselves by putting their initials in Morse code on the Green Monster.

2. Fenway is commonly known as both the smallest and the oldest of all ballparks currently in use in MLB. However, the press area inside Fenway is actually the largest in the majors, with three full rows for local, national, and other media.

3. When Daisuke Matsuzaka first showed up at Fenway to pitch in 2007, he was accompanied by a herd of Japanese journalists. However, there simply wasn't enough space for them and others in the press box. They then went to a backroom where they announced the game "live" while watching on TV.

4. The original Green Monster was completely coated with adverts back in 1947, ostensibly to pay for the cost of its construction. Soon after, it was given its first layer of "Fen Green Paint," now known as "Monster Green."

5. Arguably three of the greatest Red Sox players in their entire history, Ted Williams, Carl Yastrzemski, and Jim Rice, won a combined zero World Series rings. Williams played and lost only once in 1946, while Yaz and Rice ended up losing twice. All the deciding games of those Series went by the same score of 4-3.

6. The only Red Sox slugger to rack up more than 50 homers in a single year in the whole of the twentieth century was Jimmie Foxx in 1938.

7. The first player ever signed by the Boston Americans was Jimmy Collins in 1901. He also served as the team's manager (for the grand salary of $5,500) and recorded the franchise's first hit.

8. Pedro Martinez was invited to participate in the All-Star Game in 2002, but turned down the offer. He claimed that he wanted to be completely rested for his next start with the Sox.

9. John Valentin is the one and only player in MLB to hit for the cycle and score an unassisted triple play in his career. Valentin's two pieces of magic came in 1994 and 1996.

10. In 1999, General Manager Dan Duquette referred to Fenway Park as economically obsolete in an era of bigger and better ballparks. Obviously, he and other managers pushing for a new stadium didn't get their way, and we're still "stuck" with Fenway!

CHAPTER 10:

WHO'S ON FIRST?

QUIZ TIME!

1. Jimmie Foxx, also known as "Double-X," was imported from the Philadelphia Athletics for two players (George Savino and Gordon Rhodes) and a significant amount of cash from Boston owner Tom Yawkey's pocket. How much to be exact?

    a. $12,500
    b. $50,000
    c. $125,000
    d. $150,000

2. Foxx's 50 home runs in 1938 stood as the Sox record until another big basher did the job with his bat in 2006, smashing 54. Who was the latter batter?

    a. Trot Nixon
    b. Big Papi Ortiz
    c. Manny Ramírez
    d. Keven Youkilis

3. "You just can't imagine how far he could hit a baseball," said one of Foxx's contemporaries. Who was that player?

   a. Lou Gehrig
   b. Al Simmons
   c. Ted Williams
   d. Wilt Chamberlain

4. Boston's catcher Jimmie Foxx, also nicknamed "The Beast," was apparently so strong that opposing Yankee pitcher Lefty Gomez said, "He has muscles in his _____." What part of Foxx's anatomy was he referring to?

   a. His teeth
   b. His eyebrows
   c. His hair
   d. His knuckles

5. When Foxx drove the ball into the third deck of Yankee Stadium off Gomez, the pitcher was asked how far he thought the ball travelled. What was his reply?

   a. "I don't know—maybe all the way back to Boston."
   b. "I don't know, but I do know it took somebody 45 minutes to go up there and get it back."
   c. "I don't know, but I certainly ducked."
   d. "I don't know—perhaps there'll be a visit from the US military later."

6. When Foxx played in Philadelphia, his manager was forced to sell many of his best players including Jimmie. Why?

a. The city of Philly was suffering from a deadly virus at the time.

b. Philly's "blue laws" prevented profitable Sunday baseball until 1934.

c. Philly only allowed players who were truly athletic to play.

d. Philly's stadium was too small to support more than one star player.

7. Boston first baseman George "Boomer" Scott was born in Greenville, Mississippi. His father passed away when he was only 2, forcing George to pick cotton by his mother's side. At what age did he start picking?

a. 5

b. 7

c. 9

d. 11

8. Why was Boomer Scott kicked off his first Little League team?

a. He was "too good" at baseball.

b. His uniform didn't fit properly.

c. He was twice the size of some of the other players.

d. He didn't possess a legal birth certificate.

9. Which of his high school teams did Scott lead to state championships in Mississippi?

a. Baseball and basketball

b. Football and basketball

c. Curling and track and field

d. Baseball, basketball, and ice hockey

10. Boomer Scott exercised his great sense of humor with the Sox, as well as the Kansas City Royals and Yankees. He wore a special necklace while playing in the field. What did he claim it was made of?

a. Things he had stolen from opponents he didn't like

b. Strange items that he picked up during his climb to the Major Leagues

c. Objects that fans had thrown at him

d. Second basemen's teeth

11. Boomer Scott spent a full nine years with the Sox and leads all Boston first basemen with the most games played at that position. For how many games did he guard the bag?

a. 742

b. 866

c. 888

d. 988

12. In 1984, one opposing pitcher paid tribute to George Scott's hitting prowess by saying, "When Scott first came into the league, no one knew how to pitch to him, and they didn't find out for three years." Who was Scott's fan?

a. Tommy John

b. Clay Christiansen

c. Ron Guidry

d. Dave Righetti

13. Some pundits say that first baseman Mo Vaughan was Big Papi before Big Papi. What was broadcaster Jerry Remy's quote about Mo?

    a. "Baltimore pitchers—beware and be careful!"

    b. "He was a home run waiting to happen."

    c. "The Green Monster's in trouble."

    d. "He could break Babe's home run record very quickly."

14. Surely Mo "Hit Dog" Vaughan was an intimidating hitter, with his front elbow sometimes almost hanging in the strike zone. What was Vaughan best known for as a hitter?

    a. Being extremely patient with his pitch selection

    b. Swinging wildly at breaking balls

    c. Taking a lot of time out of the batter's box

    d. Crowding the plate

15. While playing for the New York Mets in Shea Stadium in 2002, he hit a mammoth blast that clanged off the middle of the "Bud" sign way out in center field. Approximately how far did that ball travel?

    a. 475 feet

    b. 505 feet

    c. 515 feet

    d. 525 feet

16. Boston's first baseman from 2004-2012 was Kevin Youkilis who proved to be a "big-game player" in the 2007 title sprint. What position did "Youk" start his big-league career playing?

a. Right field

b. Shortstop

c. Third base

d. Catcher

17. What was the main reason given for Kevin's trade to the White Sox in 2012?

    a. The Boston media rode him for putting on weight in the off-season.

    b. He went into a prolonged batting slump.

    c. He was tired of playing first base and requested a change.

    d. He had a major disagreement with manager Bobby Valentine.

18. What did Youkilis emphasize that good hitters always do?

    a. Good hitters walk.

    b. Good hitters keep their eyes open.

    c. Good hitters are at a premium in today's game.

    d. Good hitters typically hit the ball.

19. Mike Napoli started as a catcher but ended up covering first base as a Red Sox player in 2012. He possessed a fearsome swing, but also set the BoSox all-time single-season record for most strikeouts by a player. What other team did he also "lead" in strikeouts in a single season?

    a. Baltimore Orioles

    b. Cleveland Indians

    c. Anaheim Angels

    d. Texas Rangers

20. On Monday, April 15, 2013, Mike Napoli helped the Sox win with a walk-off double. That same day, a terrible event occurred on Patriots Day in Boston leading Big Papi to shout, "This is our f—king city!", giving some solace to the shocked population. What happened?

    a. The Boston Tea Party

    b. The Boston Marathon Bombing

    c. The Boston Celtics lost in the NBA Finals

QUIZ ANSWERS

1. D – $150,000, Equivalent to about $2,763,669 in 2019 dollars

2. B – Big Papi Ortiz

3. C – Ted Williams

4. C – His hair

5. B – "I don't know, but I do know it took somebody 45 minutes to go up there and get it back."

6. B – Philly's "blue laws" prevented profitable Sunday baseball until 1934.

7. C – 9

8. A – He was "too good" at baseball.

9. B – Football and basketball

10. D – Second basemen's teeth

11. D – 988

12. A – Tommy John

13. B – "He was a home run waiting to happen."

14. D – Crowding the plate

15. B – 505 feet

16. C – Third base

17. D – He had a major disagreement with manager Bobby Valentine.

18. A – Good hitters walk.

19. B – Cleveland Indians

20. B – The Boston Marathon Bombing

DID YOU KNOW?

1. At 6:33 in the morning the day after the bombings, BoSox player Will Middlebrooks tweeted, *"I can't wait to put on my jersey today... I get to play for the strongest city out there. #BostonStrong."* That hashtag quickly became the city's rallying cry.

2. Maybe the first great first baseman with the Red Sox was Garland "Jake" Stahl who also led the squad to victory in the 1912 World Series. In addition, Stahl was indirectly responsible for the coining of the baseball term "jaking it" (or faking injury to stay out of the lineup).

3. After arriving at Fenway following a complicated deal involving the Chunichi Dragons of Japan and the Florida Marlins, Keven Millar was a first baseman and cog as the Red Sox finally grabbed their Series rings in 2004. Millar created the phrase "Cowboy Up" and called his teammates "idiots" to keep them loose.

4. Maybe Millar's most famous quote was directed at the Yankees who should've listened better just before the Sox pulled out Game 5 in the ALCS in 2004: "Don't let us win tonight. This is a big game. They've got to win because if we win we've got Pedro coming back today and then Schilling will pitch Game 6 and then you can take that fraud stuff and put it to bed."

5. Adrian Gonzalez was a hot-hitting first baseman from

Miami when the BoSox and Theo Epstein snapped him up in late 2010. He looked set to turn into a Boston cornerstone when he signed a seven-year extension. Incredibly, he only played 282 games in Beantown before being shipped to L.A.

6. Jerry Remy gave George Scott some love when the second baseman called Boomer the best he'd ever played with. When Jerry made a bad throw, he knew there was "a damn good chance" that George would dig it out somehow. Lots of double plays were the result.

7. Our first base stories wouldn't be complete without a little more on Bill Buckner. After the fateful ball got through the infield, it was snapped up by the right field umpire Ed Montague. It made the rounds of the Mets clubhouse, inherited a tobacco stain from a kiss, bought by Charlie Sheen, and later was sold at auction for a mere $412K in 2012.

8. Though Carl Yastrzemski became famous for manning Fenway's left field, he also piled up several hundred games playing at first base. Yaz didn't seem particularly speedy, but he turned out to be a terror on the base paths, piling up 168 stolen bags.

9. Despite the fact that first baseman James Edward "Pete" Runnels played for the Sox during a down period in 1960, he was a two-time AL batting champion. He finished his career for the Houston Colt .45s (the precursor to the modern-day Astros).

10. Forget the error already—stuff happens. Before the decisive game against the Mets, Bill Buckner had made himself into an outstanding first baseman (during the regular season), smashing his own Major League record of 184 assists.

CHAPTER 11:

WHO'S GOT SECOND?

QUIZ TIME!

1. Dustin Pedroia roamed the second base grass for the Sox during their 2007 and 2013 championships and served as an unofficial coach while injured during their 2018 run. Why is he affectionately called "the Laser Show"?

   a. Because he's adept at leaping to spear line drives with his glove.
   b. Because he always invites teammates to enjoy laser shows at his home.
   c. Because of his line-drive hitting ability.
   d. Because he's a huge fan of *Star Wars*.

2. In only his first two years with the Sox, Pedroia became the only player in MLB history to win Rookie of the Year, MVP, a Gold Glove, and a World Series ring.

   a. True
   b. False

3. What is missing from the statement Dustin made about

himself when asked if he wished he were bigger: "No, I always wanted to be a miniature _____."?

    a. Tasmanian devil

    b. Badass

    c. Bad guy

    d. Second baseman

4. In his 2008 MVP season, Pedroia seemed to be vacuuming up every ball hit anywhere on the right side of the diamond. How many errors did he make that year?

    a. None

    b. Only 20 in 150 games

    c. Only 10 in 160 games

    d. Only 6 in 157 games

5. What does Dustin Pedroia, the player known as "the Laser Show" or "the Muddy Chicken," like to do in his spare time?

    a. Play backgammon

    b. Play cribbage

    c. Play darts

    d. Play Scrabble

6. Playing second base for the Sox together with the likes of Ted Williams, Johnny Pesky, and Dom DiMaggio, Bobby Doerr was an undisputed leader in the clubhouse. What did Williams call him?

    a. The silent killer

    b. Silent night

c. The silent captain

d. A silent partner

7. At one point, Boston's Bobby Doerr owned the AL record for most consecutive chances without an error. How many opportunities did he handle without a miss?

 a. 322

 b. 365

 c. 414

 d. 501

8. After becoming a Red Sox regular in 1938, his career stretched into the 1950s. Before returning as a scout in 1957, what did Doerr take time away from baseball to do?

 a. He acted briefly as a telephone equipment salesman.

 b. He tried his hand as a fishing guide.

 c. He opened a burger shop in Oregon.

 d. He tried his hand as a cattle rancher.

9. From 1947 to 1957, Billy Goodman took his turn at second as well as a number of other positions to define the role of "super-utility" player. What were the only two positions he did NOT play?

 a. Catcher and center field

 b. Pitcher and third base

 c. First and third base

 d. Shortstop and water boy

10. Goodman signed his first pro contract at the tender age of 18. Which southern team did he play for first?

a. Atlanta Braves

b. Atlanta Crackers

c. Charlotte Hornets

d. Charlotte Bobcats

11. With the team slumping after the All-Star break in 1988, Sox manager Joe Morgan inserted local product Jody Reed into the lineup. The Sox took off, and when Reed changed from shortstop to cover second, "Morgan's Magic" had arrived. What was Reed's specialty?

a. He had 10 or more sacrifice bunts in five seasons.

b. He arranged free tickets to Sox games for all his local friends.

c. He struck out in only 5% of his at-bats.

d. He was never caught in a run-down.

12. After his playing career, Jody Reed turned into a mobile manager. Which of the following teams did he NOT manage?

a. Chattanooga Lookouts

b. Gulf Coast Yankees

c. New York Yankees

d. Staten Island Yankees

13. A rookie in 1967, Mike Andrews became a key contributor at second base to the 1967 "Impossible Dream" team. After playing with several other teams following the Sox, why did he return to Boston?

a. He wanted to finish his career as a Sox.

b. He returned to head the Jimmy Fund, an agency set up to fight cancer.

c. He missed the fresh sea air of the Boston port.

d. He was hired by Harvard University to teach a class about baseball.

14. Second bagger Jerry Remy injected speed into a slow Boston squad in the late '70s. What baseball skill was he especially known for?

a. The drag bunt

b. The suicide squeeze

c. The drag queen play

d. The hidden ball play

15. Finished as a player, Jerry Remy moved quickly into broadcasting with NESN and was actually voted as the state of Massachusetts's favorite announcer in 2004. What kind of food stand does Remy also own outside Fenway?

a. A hot dog stand

b. A pizza stand

c. A popcorn stand

d. An ice cream stand

16. Remy is also the author of three baseball books and several children's books about the Red Sox mascot Wally the Green Monster.

a. True

b. False

17. Marty Barrett played second for the Sox in the '80s and came up big as the ALCS MVP in 1986. What role did Marty play in the 33-inning game between Triple-A Pawtucket and the Rochester Red Wings in 1981?

    a. He saved the Sox twice with diving catches.
    b. He pleaded with the umpire to call the game a tie.
    c. He scored the winning run.
    d. He tied the game for the Sox in the 32nd inning.

18. What was the reason for Marty's ejection from the final game of the 1990 ALCS after Roger Clemens had already been booted?

    a. He protested Roger's ejection by throwing water bottles onto the field.
    b. He called the umpire names that you wouldn't repeat at home.
    c. He sat down on the base path and refused to get up.
    d. He threw a bag of balls from the dugout onto the field.

19. Dominican second baseman Julio Lugo signed a monster $36 million deal with the Sox in 2006 and then proceeded to go 0 for 31 at the plate. But he soon got it turned around with a nice hitting and stolen base streak. What were the two streaks?

    a. 8-game hitting streak / 20 straight bases stolen
    b. 10-game hitting streak / 10 straight bases stolen
    c. 14-game hitting streak / 20 straight bases stolen
    d. 20-game hitting streak / 30 straight bases stolen

20. Brock Wyatt Holt played second base for the Sox in their winning 2018 campaign. What's his nickname?

   a. The Brock Star
   b. Keep Holtin'
   c. Brock and Roll
   d. Brockin'

QUIZ ANSWERS

1. C – Because of his line-drive hitting ability.

2. A – True

3. B – Badass, Pedroia is 5 feet 7 inches tall.

4. D – Only 6 in 157 games

5. B – Play cribbage

6. C – The silent captain

7. C – 414

8. D – He tried his hand as a cattle rancher.

9. A – Catcher and center field

10. B – Atlanta Crackers

11. A – He had 10 or more sacrifice bunts in five seasons.

12. C – New York Yankees

13. B – He returned to head the Jimmy Fund, an agency set up to fight cancer.

14. A – The drag bunt

15. A – A hot dog stand

16. A – True

17. C – He scored the winning run.

18. A – He protested Roger's ejection by throwing water bottles onto the field.

19. C – 14-game hitting streak / 20 straight bases stolen

20. A – The Brock Star

DID YOU KNOW?

1. Brock Holt has hit for the cycle twice and is the only Major Leaguer ever to do it in a postseason game. Chosen for the All-Star Game in 2015, he was the first player ever nominated who'd started at seven different positions before the break.

2. When Dustin Pedroia talked about the vagaries of his job, he made us all think twice about our future security. "I go out and break my leg next year and can't play ever again, I got 40 million dollars. Nothing's guaranteed in this world, except that 40 million dollars."

3. Denny Doyle had a two-year stint with the Sox in 1975. He's personally responsible for breaking up three no-hit bids by three different teams, including one against the San Diego Padres and ex-BoSox manager Don Zimmer. The Padres continue to be the only team in MLB history with zero no-hitters.

4. In that tremendous win by the BoSox in Game 6 of the '75 Series behind Fisk's pole-aided homer, Denny Doyle was involved in a previous play that fans still talk about today. Doyle tried to score on a shallow fly by Freddy Lynn to right but was cut down at the plate by George Foster. Manager Zimmer was yelling "no, no, no!", but the Fenway crowd noise was so loud that Doyle thought it was "go, go, go!".

5. Turning the double play at second often means the second baseman must face an on-charging runner, sometimes with cleats held high. Dustin gives us his perspective: "I hang in there all the time. I'm not afraid to be taken out. I think that's the biggest thing to do—just stay in there on the double play."

6. Alex Cora played both second and short during his career before becoming manager of the Series-winning Sox of 2018. He is also the owner of the longest-ever recorded at-bat as a Dodger, fouling off 14 straight pitches before homering. His brother Joey, watching the game in a bar, quipped that when the at-bat started, he and a friend were ordering their first beer, and at the end they were "so drunk that we had to call a cab to take us home."

7. Cora remains more famous as a Boston manager than as a player (and not only for alleged "sign-stealing"!). He became only the fifth manager ever to win the World Series in his inaugural season, and the first Puerto Rican to do so.

8. Implicated in a previous sign-stealing scheme with the Astros, Cora's name came up again in a similar situation with the Sox. At the end of the day, Alex left the BoSox, and MLB commissioner Rob Manfred suspended him for the remainder of the 2020 season. Not bad to be suspended when you're already forced to stay home…

9. Speaking of sign-stealing using technology in baseball, it's been around for a while (since about 1899 with the Phillies

to be exact). And wouldn't you know that the Red Sox and Yankees would've been involved somewhere along the line. In 1959, the use of centerfield cameras was questioned, and NBC banned such devices as a result.

10. Back at second, the aforementioned "hidden ball trick" by Marty Barrett was a rousing success, earning him the nickname "Dekemaster" by teammate Bill Buckner. "I've always played that way because I thought I had to. There are so many big guys with natural ability in the game, a guy my size is at a disadvantage. So, I've always tried to do everything I could think of to win. That's the only chance I've got," replied Barrett, at all of 5 feet 10 inches.

CHAPTER 12:

WHO'S AT THE HOT CORNER?

QUIZ TIME!

1. With third base known as the proverbial hot corner, nobody could handle the heat better than Wade Boggs. But Boggsie was most known for his bat and uncanny ability to get on base in any fashion. What was his best on-base percentage (OBP) during his 11 Sox seasons?

    a. .428

    b. .455

    c. .476

    d. .496

2. Even more incredible was that Boggs had slaved away in the Boston farm system for eight years before getting the call from "the bigs" in 1982.

    a. True

    b. False

3. As a rookie, Wade made some noise by hitting .349. How did he finally find his way into the lineup?

a. Starting third baseman Carney Lansford was mired in a slump.

b. Wade won a "home run derby" against other rookies in practice.

c. Starting third baseman Carney Lansford went down with a broken ankle.

d. Over a few beers, Wade persuaded his manager to put him in.

4. Boggs also worked hard to improve his initially weak fielding. He took hundreds of balls in practice hits off the Fungo bat of another historic handler of the Sox hot corner. Who was he?

a. Jimmy Collins

b. Johnny Pesky

c. Rico Petrocelli

d. Frank Malzone

5. "I've never seen another hitter like him in my lifetime. I guess the only guy I could compare him to would be Rod Carew," gushed one former teammate of Boggs. Who was this admirer?

a. Ellis Burks

b. Rich Gedman

c. John Henry

d. Jerry Remy

6. The very first Boston Americans third baseman was also its manager, Jimmy Collins, from 1901 to 1907. Baseball historians give Collins the nod as helping to revolutionize play at the hot corner. What did Collins do?

a. By not playing close to the bag, he brought athleticism to the position, taking pressure off the shortstop.

b. By wearing shorter pants, he was able to reach more grounders.

c. By releasing the ball faster after catching it, he became more effective.

d. By insisting on more night games, he cooled off the hot corner.

7. In a bio released on the Baseball Hall of Fame site, Collins said of himself, "They say I was the greatest third baseman, and I would like to believe it. But I don't know. There were many great third basemen in my day."

a. True

b. False

8. To this day, who is the only BoSox third baseman to have won a Gold Glove at the position?

a. Wade Boggs

b. Frank Malzone

c. Bill Mueller

d. Johnny Pesky

9. In 1957, Frankie Malzone belted a career-high 103 RBIs. In which of the following categories did he NOT lead all AL third baggers?

a. Assists

b. Games

c. Putouts

d. Triple plays

10. After his career at the hot corner wound down, Malzone became a heralded hitting instructor. What's named after him at the team's spring training complex in Winter Haven, FL?

    a. A playing field
    b. A dressing room
    c. A snack bar
    d. A water fountain

11. Boston had to find a trusty replacement for Collins at third in 1908, and they did in Larry Gardner. What New England state known for cheddar cheese and maple syrup did Gardner hail from?

    a. Alaska
    b. Connecticut
    c. Maine
    d. Vermont

12. All that cheese helped Larry Gardner hit only 16 home runs in a decade with Boston. But one of them broke the backs of their Brooklyn opponents in the 1916 Series. What was Brooklyn's full team name?

    a. Brooklyn Dodgers
    b. Brooklyn Nets
    c. Brooklyn Robins
    d. Bronx Bombers

13. Mike Lowell was a superb defender at third for Boston and ended up winning the Series MVP in 2007. His right-

handed pulling ability was perfect for Fenway. How did he come to the Sox?

a. He was the "throw-in" player who came with Josh Beckett from the Marlins.
b. He and "a player to be named later" were traded for Josh Beckett.
c. He was found drinking at a bar near Fenway.
d. He was picked up "on waivers."

14. Even though a right hip injury slowed him permanently in 2008, Mike Lowell was a certified fan favorite. What was the "style" that the Fenway faithful were attracted by?

a. His brilliant style of bunting
b. His blue-collar style
c. His disco style
d. His hard-driving style

15. Bill Mueller also fielded at third for the Sox and turned into the AL batting champ in 2003. During the enchanted 2004 season, Mueller also came up clutch against which formidable reliever?

a. Brandon Duckworth
b. Chad Durbin
c. Alan Embree
d. Mariano Rivera

16. Even though Carney Lansford won a batting title while playing third for the Sox in 1981, why's that season accompanied by an asterisk?

a. It was shortened by an earthquake affecting L.A. and San Francisco.

b. It was shortened by a strike.

c. It was cut short by an umpire walkout.

d. It was shortened due to riots in L.A.

17. Adrián Beltré graced third base for the Red Sox in 2010 and is one of a handful of big leaguers to have hit more than 100 round-trippers for more than three teams. What city did he come from in the Dominican Republic?

a. Santo Domingo Este

b. Santo Domingo Oeste

c. Santo Domingo

d. Santiago de los Caballeros

18. Continuing with the recent Dominican domination of third base in Boston, how old was Rafael "Carita" Devers when the Red Sox signed him as a free agent?

a. 12

b. 14

c. 16

d. 19

19. As truly the first of many talented Boston third basemen, Jimmy Collins deserves special mention. "Third base was put into baseball for Collins," said his contemporary Bill Coughlin, who also manned the hot corner. Which two teams did Coughlin play for?

a. Detroit Tigers and Washington Senators

b. Detroit Pistons and Washington Bullets

c. Detroit Tigers and New York Highlanders

d. Detroit Lions and New York Knickerbockers

20. Washington Senators owner and Hall of Fame executive Clark Griffith remarked that Jimmy Collins was like a _____ on bunts. To which feline was he referring?

a. A bobcat

b. A cat

c. A cheetah

d. A panther

QUIZ ANSWERS

1. C – .476

2. B – False, He had slaved away for six years in the Boston farm system.

3. C – Starting third baseman Carney Lansford went down with a broken ankle.

4. B – Johnny Pesky

5. D – Jerry Remy

6. A – By not playing close to the bag, he brought athleticism to the position, taking pressure off the shortstop.

7. A – True

8. B – Frank Malzone

9. D – Triple plays

10. A – A playing field

11. D – Vermont

12. C – Brooklyn Robins

13. A – He was the "throw-in" player who came with Josh Beckett from the Marlins.

14. B – His blue-collar style

15. D – Mariano Rivera

16. B – It was shortened by a strike.

17. C – Santo Domingo

18. C – 16

19. A – Detroit Tigers and Washington Senators

20. B – A cat

DID YOU KNOW?

1. In only his second Major League game on April 20, 1895, Jimmy Collins was designated to play in the outfield alongside High Duffy and Tommy McCarthy of the Boston Beaneaters. All three would go on to Hall of Fame glory.

2. Collins finished his career in Boston with the remark, "I gave everything I had to baseball, and when I quit, I was like the guy who died with his boots on."

3. Frank Malzone was born in Brooklyn and planned to be an electrician if baseball didn't work out. He signed with the Red Sox for $150 a month in 1947.

4. It's hard to imagine the one and only Carl Yastrzemski ever struggling, but he said this of Malzone, "When I first came to the big leagues in 1961, Frank was the guy who took me under his wing, I struggled when I first came up, and he took care of me and stayed with me. I owe him a lot. He was a real class guy, a very caring guy, and I owe him a lot. You aren't going to find too many people like him."

5. Larry Gardner's Vermont hometown lies only 16 miles from the Canadian border. Despite a population of around 2,000 inhabitants, Enosburg Falls proclaims itself the "Dairy Center of the World." Larry captained his high school ice hockey team in the early 1900s, but he admitted that baseball was the town's favorite sport.

6. As a high school pitcher, Gardner squeezed out a win on a game-ending double play, home to first. The town of Enosburg Falls, Vermont, celebrated the boys' fourth shutout of the season with a band concert, a bonfire, and a promenade. The losing opponents from Montpelier stayed overnight to enjoy the good times.

7. Johnny Pesky had a unique perspective on what it was to be victorious. "When you win, you eat better, sleep better, and your beer tastes better. And your wife looks like Gina Lollobrigida," he claimed.

8. Pesky also had a peculiar outlook on the fickle life of a Major Leaguer (or a player at any level, for that matter). "Baseball can build you up to the sky one day and the next day you have to climb a stepladder to look up at a snake," he mused.

9. Popular Boston player "Youk" was presented with the following headline back in November 2018: "The Kevin Youkilis Story: Why The Former Fat Third Baseman Deserves Red Sox MVP."

10. Kevin Youkilis received an apt nickname, "Euclis: The Greek God of Walks," in the best-selling book, *Moneyball: The Art of Winning an Unfair Game*, later turned into a major movie starring none other than Brad Pitt as the Oakland A's manager.

CHAPTER 13:

WHO'S AT SHORT?

QUIZ TIME!

1. Though he never won the World Series outright as a Red Sox, Nomar Garciaparra is considered one of the greatest shortstops ever for the team. What BoSox mark for right-handers did he set?

    a. His back-to-back AL batting titles

    b. His 44 doubles as a rookie

    c. His .372 batting average

    d. His ability to slam pitches outside the strike zone

2. What decision by BoSox management in December of 2003 left Nomar less than enthused?

    a. They made a move to acquire Alex Rodriguez.

    b. They made a move to trade for Willie Bloomquist.

    c. They tried to sign Deivi Cruz.

    d. They tried to ban Nomar's wife from the clubhouse.

3. What sleight of batting hand was Garciaparra the only player to ever achieve in his home stadium?

a. He ripped two grand slam homers in the same game.

b. He hit four triples in the same game.

c. He hit for the cycle in three consecutive games.

d. He once knocked in five runs as Boston beat New York, 5-0.

4. Before reaching the Red Sox and Fenway Park in 1996, which of the following teams did Nomar NOT play for?

   a. Billings Buffaloes

   b. Pawtucket Red Sox

   c. Sarasota Red Sox

   d. Trenton Thunder

5. BoSox shortstop Joe Cronin may have been slightly overshadowed by the likes of Ted Williams and Jimmie Foxx. However, on June 17, 1943, Cronin became the first player in history to hit pinch-hit homers in both games of a doubleheader.

   a. True

   b. False

6. Joe Cronin wasn't just a player. Which of the following roles did Cronin NOT fulfill during his baseball career?

   a. American League president

   b. General manager

   c. Pennant-winning manager

   d. National League president

7. Why did Cronin spend most of his young life in poverty-stricken conditions?

a. His father was disabled and unable to find work.

b. The 1906 San Francisco Earthquake destroyed what his family owned.

c. His family were victims of the Great Depression.

d. Many of his relatives were infected with the Spanish Flu.

8. After the 1947 season, Cronin was hired as the Red Sox general manager. Which of the players below did NOT help the Red Sox challenge for AL pennants in two consecutive years (1948-1949)?

a. Spud Chandler

b. Ellis Kinder

c. Jack Kramer

d. Vern Stephens

9. What record did the inimitable Rico Petrocelli set for shortstops in 1969 that still stands today?

a. He hit safely in 42 games.

b. He signed autographs for at least an hour after every home game.

c. He handled 75 chances without an error.

d. He hammered 40 homers.

10. What reason did Jerry Remy cite Rico being another "perfect hitter" for Fenway Park?

a. His uppercut swing launched many round-trippers.

b. As a rightie, he was a dead pull hitter.

c. He often professed his love of the Green Monster.

d. He rarely struck out.

11. Rick "Rooster" Burleson was the shortstop involved in the 1975 slugfest that saw the BoSox finally fall in seven to the Reds. Which was the team that originally drafted Rick, but he refused to sign with?

   a. California Angels
   b. Milwaukee Brewers
   c. Minnesota Twins
   d. Texas Rangers

12. Who is the following quote attributed to: "Some guys didn't like to lose, but Rick got angry if the score was even tied."?

   a. Bill "Spaceman" Lee
   b. Carlton "Pudge" Fisk
   c. Butch Hobson
   d. Dick Drago

13. Despite his contribution to the Red Sox over the years, Burleson started his big-league career by tying a record for futility. What was it?

   a. He struck out six times.
   b. He booted the ball three times.
   c. He was caught stealing twice.
   d. He missed the cutoff man three times.

14. Following his playing career, Burleson was a baserunning instructor and also had a hand in managing numerous teams. Which of the following did he NOT manage?

   a. Lancaster JetHawks
   b. Louisville Cardinals

c. San Antonio Missions

d. San Bernardino Stampede

15. Édgar Rentería played short for Boston in 2004, but he's better known for making the final out as a Card against Keith Foulkes as the BoSox got their rings earlier that year. Born in Colombia, what is Edgar's nickname?

    a. The Barranquilla Baby

    b. The Cartagena Kid

    c. The Medellín Magician

    d. The Bogotá Bad Boy

16. In 1999, Team Rentería, which consisted of Édgar and his two brothers Edinson and Evert, started the Colombian Professional Baseball League. The league still exists today although the 2010-2011 season was cancelled due to especially bad weather.

    a. True

    b. False

17. Jed Lowrie played for three minor league teams from 2005-2007, was named the Portland Sea Dogs' MVP, and was called up to play shortstop with the BoSox in 2008. How many games did he appear in with no errors?

    a. 40

    b. 49

    c. 65

    d. 80

18. Born in New Mexico while his parents were on the go from Oklahoma to California, Vern Stephens was elected

to the Boston Red Sox Hall of Fame in 2006. One of the hardest-hitting shortstops in ML history, what was Vern's nickname?

a. The Second Bambino
b. The Little Slug
c. The Little Stallion
d. The Big Vernster

19. Stephens decided to break with American League baseball and headed south to Mexico where he signed a five-year deal. What happened next?

a. He was unable to adapt to life in Mexico and decided to go to Panama.
b. He decided to return to the U.S. due to the extreme Mexican heat.
c. His father (an umpire) and a Browns scout drove to Mexico and brought him back.
d. His mother called him and persuaded him to return to California.

20. John Valentin's best year at short for the BoSox was in 1995 when he batted .298, blasted 27 homers, 37 doubles, and stole 20 bases. After his playing days, he bounced around as a manager, including one stint in New Mexico. What was his team's name?

a. Albuquerque Antelopes
b. Albuquerque Isotopes
c. Santa Fe Sentinels
d. Santa Fe Sandals

QUIZ ANSWERS

1. C – His .372 batting average

2. A – They made a move to acquire Alex Rodriguez.

3. A – He ripped two grand slam homers in the same game.

4. A – Billings Buffaloes

5. A – True

6. D – National League president

7. B – The 1906 San Francisco Earthquake destroyed what his family owned.

8. A – Spud Chandler

9. D – He hammered 40 homers.

10. B – As a rightie, he was a dead pull hitter.

11. C – Minnesota Twins

12. A – Bill "Spaceman" Lee

13. B – He booted the ball three times. (In other words, he had three errors.)

14. B – Louisville Cardinals

15. A – The Barranquilla Baby

16. A – True

17. B – 49

18. B – The Little Slug

19. C – His father (an umpire) and a Browns scout drove to Mexico and brought him back.

20. B – Albuquerque Isotopes

DID YOU KNOW?

1. You might expect that the tiny islands of Aruba and Curacao would only produce one outstanding baseball player who the Red Sox managed to snap up: Xander Bogaerts. In fact, the islands' even more famous baseball citizen was Andruw Jones, who blasted 434 ML homers, mainly with the Braves, and another 50 in Japan.

2. Bogaerts also has a twin brother, Jair, who was signed by the Sox as an international free agent. Being born in Aruba allowed Xander to take the field for the Netherlands in the 2011 World Baseball Classic, which the team won.

3. Xander Bogaerts and Mookie Betts were the first pair of Red Sox teammates to score 100 runs or more before the tender age of 24 since 1942.

4. Garciaparra made a series of adjustments every time he stepped into or out of the batter's box (making some pitchers' days much longer than expected). One reason for these batting "tics" may have been his childhood idol. "Back then, my idol was Bugs Bunny, because I saw a cartoon of him playing ball—you know, the one where he plays every position himself with nobody else on the field but him? Now that I think of it, Bugs is still my idol. You have to love a ballplayer like that," Nomar recalls.

5. "When I go home, my mother still makes me take out the garbage," Garciaparra reminisced, perhaps coming close

to how pro players maintain their modesty despite their many millions.

6. Shortstop Johnny Pesky was with the Red Sox organization in some capacity for 61 of his 73 years in pro ball. He was also the subject of a book entitled *The Teammates* by David Halberstam, featuring fellow Sox Ted Williams, Dom DiMaggio, and Bobby Doerr.

7. Pesky was originally from Portland, OR, and played for the Silverton Red Sox, which happened to be owned by the Silver Falls Timber and Tom Yawkey, the big Red Sox boss. A skilled hockey player, Pesky had a workout with the Boston Bruins.

8. The right field foul line at Fenway is marked by the massive "Pesky Pole," even though Johnny (a light-hitting contact hitter) only managed 16 homers in 4,745 at-bats in the Major Leagues. Former teammate and Red Sox announcer Mel Parnell named the pole after his pal.

9. Venezuelan Alex Gonzalez, another top defensive shortstop in a Sox uniform, goes through a prayer ritual before every game to maintain focus and also the memory of one of his sons who remained in a coma for two years in a Miami hospital.

10. In 1984, BoSox shortstop Jackie Gutiérrez appeared on the Topps (of baseball trading card fame) All-Star Rookie team as did José Iglesias, another Sox shortstop, in 2013.

CHAPTER 14:

THE OUTFIELD GANG

QUIZ TIME!

1. Tris Speaker, considered one of the greatest defensive centerfielders in history, was also pretty handy with the bat. What is his ML record for career doubles?

    a. 684

    b. 725

    c. 792

    d. 833

2. In 1909, what was Speaker's fielding glove referred to by players and the press?

    a. "Where the ball has no escape"

    b. "Where triples go to die"

    c. "Where the streets have no name"

    d. "Where the lost ones go"

3. Before he became one of the top Red Sox outfielders of all time, Speaker suffered a football injury in 1905. What happened to his arm in the accident?

a. It was sprained so badly that he lost his job on a ranch.

b. It turned such brilliant black and blue colors that a local artist painted it.

c. It was broken in three places.

d. It almost had to be amputated.

4. When Duffy Lewis took charge of left field in 1910, Fenway featured a steep incline going back to the wall. After becoming so skilled at handling the incline, how was Duffy pictured by local cartoonists in the papers?

a. He was shown as a mountain climber making catches amid sheep and snowcaps.

b. He was shown as a skydiver making the catch amid mountain peaks.

c. He was pictured rappelling amid steep cliffs making the catch.

d. He was pictured as a race car driver making catches on a mountain road.

5. Around 1910, Harry Hooper joined Duffy Lewis and Tris Speaker with the Red Sox to form one of the best outfield trios in baseball history. What was this outfield gang called?

a. The Graying Eagles

b. The Golden Glovers

c. The Golden Outfield

d. The Golden Triangle

6. Hooper was born in Bell Station, California, on August 24, 1887. Why had his family migrated to California along with many others?

    a. To purchase inexpensive land on the San Andreas Fault Line
    b. To take advantage of the US government's Western Relocation Program
    c. To take advantage of the many job opportunities in Silicon Valley
    d. To take advantage of the California Gold Rush

7. After one year in the NFL with the San Francisco 49ers, Carroll Hardy chose baseball, and the Red Sox chose him. He is the only player in the history of the game to pinch-hit for Ted Williams, Carl Yastrzemski, and finally Roger Maris.

    a. True
    b. False

8. Dominic "Dom" DiMaggio, also known as "The Little Professor," played his entire career for the Red Sox from 1940 to 1953. Who were his two, professional ball-playing brothers?

    a. Jimmy and Joey
    b. Joe and Vince
    c. Sammy and Tony
    d. Vinny and Victor

9. Dom was the youngest of nine children as well as two other brothers who played in the Major Leagues. What position did all of them take to?

a. Shortstop

b. Second base

c. Center field

d. Designated hitter

10. Reggie Smith patrolled the outfield for the Sox from 1966-1973 and was known for having one of the strongest arms in baseball in his prime. What minor league team did he play for that had the same name as a hockey team?

a. Boston Bruins

b. Montreal Canadiens

c. Toronto Maple Leafs

d. Los Angeles Kings

11. Theodore "Ted" Williams, the most famous Red Sox outfielder, had his 19-year career interrupted by to wars (WWII and the Korean War). Which of the following was NOT one of his nicknames?

a. The Thumper

b. Take Me Out to the Ballpark Teddy

c. Teddy Ballgame

d. The Splendid Splinter

12. With all 19 of his years blasting the ball in Fenway, Williams finished his career with a .344 batting average, 520 home runs, and .482 on-base percentage (OBP).

a. True

b. False

13. Also inducted into the IGFA Fishing Hall of Fame, how

old was Williams when he won his last two AL batting titles (his fifth and sixth)?

    a. 34 and 35 years old

    b. 36 and 37 years old

    c. 39 and 40 years old

    d. 43 and 44 years old

14. Yet another top-notch outfielder who played only for the Sox his entire career (23 years), Carl Yastrzemski is an eight-time All-Star, a proud member of the 3,000-hit club, and the winner of seven Gold Gloves. What were his Polish parents' names?

    a. Carl Yastrzemski Sr. and Hattie Skonieczny

    b. Carl Yastrzemski Sr. and Harley Schoolczny

    c. Cal Yastrzemski Sr. and Hattie Skonieczny

    d. Cal Yastrzemski Sr. and Harriet Skonieczshy

15. Sweet-swinging Freddy Lynn took control of center field in Fenway from 1975 on. He produced an other-worldly season in '75, including the Rookie of the Year and MVP. Which other player matched his feat in 2001?

    a. Barry Bonds

    b. Hideki Matsui

    c. Ichiro Suzuki

    d. Miguel Tejada

16. What were Lynn and fellow outfield great Jim Rice referred to as?

    a. The Octopus Outfielders

    b. The Gold Dust Twins

c. The Golden Arms

d. The Golden Guns

17. Freddy was often injured by his fearless play, crashing into the Green Monster and cracking his ribs, breaking up double plays and hurting his knee. In fact, what was the most games he ever played in a single season?

a. 120

b. 130

c. 140

d. 150

18. Jim Rice roamed the Red Sox outfield for his entire 16-year MLB career. Which other famed player did he join after leading the majors in total bases for three years running?

a. Hank Aaron

b. Willie Mays

c. Ty Cobb

d. Stan Musial

19. For more than 10 years (from 1975-1986), Rice led the AL in every imaginable offensive and defensive category. In which of the following stats was he NOT the undisputed leader?

a. Suicide squeeze attempts

b. Outfield assists

c. Runs scored

d. Total games played

20. Dwight "Dewey" Evans starred alongside Rice for his entire career and played the second most games ever of

any player in Boston, behind only Yaz. Despite his glittering stats over 19 years, Dewey was never elected to the prestigious Hall of Fame (mainly due to the presence of Nolan Ryan, George Brett, and Carlton Fisk on the 1999 ballot).

a. True
b. False

QUIZ ANSWERS

1. C – 792

2. B – "Where triples go to die"

3. D – It almost had to be amputated.

4. A – He was shown as a mountain climber making catches amid sheep and snowcaps.

5. C – The Golden Outfield

6. D – To take advantage of the California Gold Rush

7. A – True

8. B – Joe and Vince

9. C – Center field

10. C – Toronto Maple Leafs

11. B – Take Me Out to the Ballpark Teddy

12. B – False, He had 521 home runs in his career.

13. C – 39 and 40 years old

14. A – Carl Yastrzemski Sr. and Hattie Skonieczny

15. C – Ichiro Suzuki

16. B – The Gold Dust Twins

17. D – 150

18. C – Ty Cobb

19. A – Suicide squeeze attempts

20. A – True

DID YOU KNOW?

1. Dwight Evans surely enjoyed Opening Day as he crushed four homers on the occasion over the years. One came on the very first pitch (April 7, 1986) and happened to be the first in the MLB that year, giving Evans the record for earliest home run hit in a season (tied in 2018 by Ian Happ).

2. At one point booed by Boston fans for his low BA, Venezuelan Tony Armas blasted off in 1984, leading the AL in homers, RBIs, and extra-base hits. Baseball ran in the Armas family blood with Tony's brother Marcos making a (slight) mark with the A's and his son Tony Jr. pitching for the Expos/Nationals, Mets, and Pirates.

3. Dave "Hendu" Henderson replaced Armas in center for the Sox and hit one of the biggest homers in Sox history in 1986. One strike from elimination, he went deep in the ninth against the Angels, and Boston reached the Series. Hendu's drive was accompanied by Al Michaels on TV: "You're looking at one for the ages here!"

4. Henderson admitted, "I was a lot better at football. I don't know why I chose baseball." But Seattle's $100K bonus offer far surpassed any scholarships from the various universities pursuing him to play pigskin. Playing center for the M's years later, he was known for chatting with fans in the outfield bleachers, even between pitches.

5. Prior to each at-bat, centerfielder Jackie Bradley Jr. writes the initials "M.S." in the batter's box dirt. They're to remind him of best friend Matt Saye who perished in a car crash. "You never know what the next day will bring, if there is a next day," Bradley ruminated.

6. In 2019, metrics showed that Bradley had the fastest reaction but selected the "worst route" of any AL centerfielder. Yet his over-the-wall catch of a blast by Trey Mancini was voted as the best in the MLB Network's Top 100 Plays for the year.

7. Gabe Kapler, Boston outfielder in 2004 and later Phillies manager, was nicknamed "The Body" due to his love of weightlifting and his ultra-low body fat count. He and his wife set up the Gabe Kapler Foundation to educate the public on domestic violence.

8. Outfield man Grady Sizemore was seized by the Sox in January 2014, and had the chance to make up to $6 million from a contract heavy on incentives. He was named the starting centerfielder in March ahead of Jackie Bradley Jr. Then, just like that, the Sox released him in June. His brief bid in Boston netted him $1.25 million.

9. Manuel "Manny" Ramírez formed a formidable batting tandem with Big Papi Ortiz from 2000-2008. Born in the Dominican Republic, Manny grew up a stone's throw from Yankee Stadium in the Bronx. But he looked the other way—in fact, all the way to Toronto, rooting for the Blue Jays and their Dominican stars, George Bell and Tony Fernández.

10. One fine day—April 22, 2007, to be exact—Manny was the first of four BoSox batters to homer against the Yankees' Chase Wright, tying a Major League record. A week later, Ramírez became the fifth Red Sox in history to clear the fences 50 times versus the rival Yanks.

CHAPTER 15:

THE HEATED RIVALRIES

QUIZ TIME!

1. The first hint of baseball rivalry arose in 1901 when Ban Johnson, owner of the Western League, decided to challenge the established National League by putting a franchise called the "Americans" in Boston, rather than Buffalo. What was the name of the pre-existing Boston club?

    a. Boston Beans

    b. Boston Blues

    c. Boston Braves

    d. Boston Celtics

2. After winning their first World Series against the Pirates in 1903, the Americans found themselves in a dog fight with the fledgling New York Highlanders who had to win a home doubleheader on the last day of the season to grab the pennant. But a spitball got away from New York's Jack Chesbro, and Boston battered New York!

a. True

b. False

3. The Red Sox bats cooled until 1912 when they put together a galaxy of stars like Tris Speaker, Duffy Lewis, Harry Hooper, and Smoky Joe Wood to take the World again. Who was their rival in that Series?

   a. New Haven Elis

   b. New York Giants

   c. New York Highlanders

   d. New York Yankees

4. Prior to the sale of the Babe, and that whole silly curse thing, the Red Sox won a final Series in 1918. Which rival fell by the wayside in that Series?

   a. Chicago Cubs

   b. Chicago White Stockings

   c. Chicago Fire

   d. Pittsburgh Pirates

5. During the last 100 years, since the American League Pennant came to exist, the New York Yankees have won the most flags ahead of Boston. Which of the following teams is NOT in the top five in terms of total pennants?

   a. Baltimore Orioles

   b. Detroit Tigers

   c. Oakland Athletics

   d. Seattle Mariners

6. It's said that the rivalry between the BoSox and the

Yankees is one of the fiercest in all American sports. What's another name given to this ongoing feud?

   a. "The Clash of the Hardball Titans"
   b. "The Greatest Rivalry on Earth"
   c. "The Northeast Slugfest"
   d. "The War of the Worlds"

7. In fact, the Red Sox had an impressive streak of wins going against their archrivals, the Yankees, back in the 1911-12 season. How many games in a row did Boston beat New York at that time?

   a. 10
   b. 13
   c. 17
   d. 22

8. Not only was Babe Ruth's sale by BoSox owner Frazee polemical. In 1923, the Sox sold another ace pitcher, Herb Pennock, to the Yanks for three players and $50K in cash. He immediately helped the Yanks win big. What was the name of one of the players sold to the Sox?

   a. Waite Hoyt
   b. Sad Sam Jones
   c. Camp Skinner
   d. Lefty O'Doul

9. Imagine being in a heated rivalry and your opponent comes to your house and wallops you. The Red Sox did just that in the 2018 ALCS on their way to the Series. What was the score of that romp in Yankee Stadium?

a. 9-1

b. 13-1

c. 16-1

d. 20-2

10. Extensive media coverage is guaranteed for any Boston-New York matchup. Red Sox-Yankees games are some of the most watched of all MLB affairs. In what year did the Red Sox make baseball history and come back from an "insurmountable" 0-3 deficit in the ALCS to reach the Series?

a. 1975

b. 1986

c. 2004

d. 2007

11. Founded in 1630, Boston was considered by many the artistic, cultural, educational, and economic power of the United States for at least 100 years. New York was looked down on as "the upstart, over-populated, dirty cousin."

a. True

b. False

12. Traditionally in baseball there are some particular plays that increase the rivalry between teams. Which of the following is NOT considered a move guaranteed to stir up "bad blood"?

a. Sliding hard at second base to break up a double play

b. Throwing "behind" a hitter

c. Intentionally hitting a batter with a pitch

d. Employing the "hidden ball trick"

13. In 2017, one prominent AL East manager shed some light on why the intra-division rivalries can get so heated: "You're in the same spring training—the Yankees, Toronto, Tampa, Boston. You're in the same leagues in the minor leagues, for the most part. You play each other 18, 20 times a year. There's no secrets, and people care." Who was the manager in question?

    a. Buck Showalter
    b. Alex Cora
    c. Don Mattingly
    d. Joe Torre

14. Perhaps ethnic tension had something to do with baseball rivalry in the past as well. About what year did the number of German-Americans surpass Irish-Americans in the Major Leagues?

    a. 1890
    b. 1900
    c. 1920
    d. 1940

15. The intense rivalries have led to player and fan fights through the decades. Even the team mascots get into the act. Which rival mascot has attacked Boston's Wally the Green Monster?

    a. The Phillie Phanatic
    b. Kansas City Royals' Sluggerrr
    c. Tampa Bay Rays' Raymond
    d. The San Diego Chicken

16. When asked to aptly describe the rivalry between the Red Sox and Yankees, a sportswriter once wrote it was much like the rivalry "between a hammer and a nail."

    a. True
    b. False

17. On May 30, 1938, Red Sox player-manager Joe Cronin and Yankee outfielder Jake Powell fought on the field and under the stands. How many people packed Yankee Stadium at the time to witness the fireworks?

    a. 65,224
    b. 71,982
    c. 83,533
    d. 92,675

18. 18. There's nothing quite like a "bench-clearing brawl" involving players and coaches to define a baseball rivalry. In 1976, two fights erupted in one game, the second involving BoSox pitcher Bill Lee and the Yankees' Craig Nettles. How many games did Lee miss from the separated shoulder he suffered in the scrap?

    a. 32
    b. 51
    c. 65
    d. He was out for the rest of the season.

19. When the Red Sox marched past the Yankees in 1986 to then face the New York Mets, the New York media had a field day, assigning numerous funny phrases to describe the Series. Which of the following was NOT one of them?

a. "A woeful day for Yankee fans"

b. "The World Series that is the Yankee nightmare"

c. "Steinbrenner's nightmare"

d. "The Red Sox Rule Series"

20. Wade Boggs could be forgiven for his excitement at finally winning the World Series with the Yanks in 1996 after trying for 18 years, mostly with the Red Sox. What action left him less in favor with BoSox fans?

a. He repeatedly kissed the Yankee logo on his uniform.

b. He jumped on the horse of a NYPD officer to celebrate.

c. He sang "New York, New York" over the PA system.

d. He mugged for numerous photos in a Statue of Liberty pose.

QUIZ ANSWERS

1. C – Boston Braves

2. A – True

3. B – New York Giants

4. A – Chicago Cubs

5. D – Seattle Mariners

6. B – "The Greatest Rivalry on Earth"

7. C – 17

8. C – Camp Skinner

9. C – 16-1

10. C – 2004

11. A – True

12. D – Employing the "hidden ball trick"

13. A – Buck Showalter

14. B – 1900

15. C – Tampa Bay Rays' Raymond

16. A – True

17. C – 83,533

18. B – 51

19. D – "The Red Sox Rule Series"

20. B – He jumped on the horse of a NYPD officer to celebrate.

DID YOU KNOW?

1. Boston's Jason Varitek and Alex "A-Rod" Rodriguez got into quite a scuffle after the latter was drilled by Bronson Arroyo's pitch on July 24, 2004. A mere two years later, Tek and A-Rod were teammates in the World Baseball Classic and got taped next to each other before a game. Tek recalls, "We never spoke a word about it. We never acknowledged it. We never acted like we didn't like each other, but we weren't going to act friendly either."

2. When world chess champion Gary Kasparov was asked if he liked his rival Anatoly Karpov, he snorted, "Do the Yankees like the Red Sox?"

3. Even MLB commissioner Bud Selig chipped in about one of sports' enduring rivalries: "You can talk about the Dodgers and Giants, the Cardinals and Cubs, the Packers and the Bears, Ohio State-Michigan, but there's nothing like the Red Sox and the Yankees."

4. Do you know what Curt Schilling said just after signing his monumental Red Sox contract in 2004? "I guess I hate the Yankees now."

5. In 2008, Yankees owner George Steinbrenner criticized the Red Sox saying, "'Red Sox Nation'? What a bunch of (expletive) that is!" He was immediately inducted into the Red Sox Nation by Red Sox principal owner John W. Henry.

6. The 2015 edition of the historic rivalry between the Sox and Yanks started on April 10 with one of the longest games in MLB history, which lasted a mere 6 hours and 49 minutes. The Yanks tied it in the bottom of the 9th, 14th, and 16th innings. Boston pulled it out, 6-5.

7. Despite the heated rivalry between the two clubs, there's a measure of respect. When Yankee great Derek Jeter announced his retirement (welcomed by most BoSox fans), Big Papi of all people was gushing. "He is one of the baseball players that I can tell you that pretty much his whole career has done everything perfectly right. And when I watch him play, I get goose bumps," Ortiz concluded.

8. The early-season brawl between the Red Sox and Yankees in 2018 became a trending topic on Twitter and one of the most viewed videos on YouTube.

9. Manager Joe McCarthy came out of retirement in 1948 to join the Red Sox. For what reason? Due to a feud with the ownership of his former team—the New York Yankees, to be precise.

10. Even the fierce rivalry took a back seat when the World Trade Center attacks occurred in September 2001. Red Sox fans held up signs that read: "Boston Loves New York." Take it easy.

CONCLUSION

The great Red Sox names roll off your tongue: Ruth, Rico, Roger, Ramírez, Tris, and Cy, even Frazee... The man who "mistakenly" sold the Bambino, Babe Ruth, to the archrival Yankees and started an 86-year rollercoaster ride as the Sox constantly battled for a world championship, which finally arrived in 2004. Now you're sitting pretty with four championships in rapid succession so far in the twenty-first century.

And here you have it: an amazing collection of Boston Red Sox trivia, information, and statistics at your fingertips! Regardless of how you fared on the quizzes, we hope you found this book entertaining, enlightening, and educational.

Ideally, you knew many of these details already, but also learned a good deal more about the history of the BoSox, their players, coaches, managers, and some of the quirky stories surrounding the team, its history, and its special stadium. If you got a little peek into the colorful details that make being a fan so much more enjoyable, then our mission was accomplished!

The good news is the trivia does not have to stop there.

Spread the word. Challenge your fellow Red Sox fans to see if they can do any better. Share some of the stories with the next generation to help them become Boston supporters too.

If you are a big enough BoSox fan, consider creating your own quiz with some of the details you know were not presented here. Then test your friends to see if they can match your knowledge.

The Boston Red Sox are one of baseball's most storied franchises. They have a long history, with many periods of success, and a few that were a bit less than successful. They've had glorious superstars, iconic moments, and hilarious tales… but most of all, they have wonderful, passionate fans. Thank you for being one of them.

Made in the USA
Monee, IL
11 December 2021

84910086R00098